Praise for

THE WAY OF THE FEARLESS WRITER

"In *The Way of the Fearless Writer*, Beth Kempton uses a Buddhist sensitivity to create a path at the intersection of our inner life, our daily life, and the lifelong practices of opening and listening; all in the service of the deeper expressive journey which, if we are true to it, gives us access to the life below. Walk with Beth on this path and the vow to write will bring your depth to the surface and your voice into the world."
—Mark Nepo, author of *Surviving Storms* and *The Book of Awakening*

"This book is an invitation to explore the writer within through the steady and soulful prompts of Beth Kempton. She taps into ancient Eastern wisdom to reveal the way to our fearless and creative self."
—Sheila Darcey, founder of SketchPoetic and author of *Sketch By Sketch*

"Beth's approach is practical and honest, yet deeply spiritual and caring. *The Way of the Fearless Writer* is a tonic for the soul. All writers should take time to read it. We're keeping this book by our bedside. It is more than just a book, it's a way of life."
—London Writers' Salon

"Are you a writer, and if so do you live in fear? If yes and yes are your answers to this double question, then you need *The Way of the Fearless Writer*." —The *Times Literary Supplement* (TLS)

"*The Way of the Fearless Writer* is a radical departure from traditional advice, allowing readers to sink into the act and art of creation— the place where formlessness meets form. A must-read for those wanting to write from an embodied sense of self."
—Steph Jagger, author of *Unbound* and *Everything Left to Remember*

"Beth Kempton is the real deal. No fluff, pure substance. *The Way of the Fearless Writer* is a liberating and life-giving book that will help you create a deeply meaningful writing life."
—Kate Eckman, broadcast journalist and author of *The Full Spirit Workout*

ALSO BY BETH KEMPTON

Freedom Seeker
Live More. Worry less. Do what you love.

Wabi Sabi
Japanese wisdom for a perfectly imperfect life

Calm Christmas and a Happy New Year
A little book of festive joy

We Are in This Together
Finding hope and opportunity in the depths of adversity

Courses (at dowhatyouloveforlife.com)

Living the Way of the Fearless Writer
Excavate Your Life
Sacred Mornings
Essence: Writing for Yogis
The Book Proposal Masterclass
Words Heal
Do What You Love
How to be Happy, Calm, Organized and Focused
Summer Writing Sanctuary
Winter Writing Sanctuary

Podcasts

The Fearless Writer Podcast
The Calm Christmas Podcast
The Freedom Seeker Podcast

Song (co-written with Danni Nicholls)

"The River"

BETH KEMPTON

THE WAY OF THE FEARLESS WRITER

MINDFUL WISDOM
FOR A FLOURISHING WRITING LIFE

ST. MARTIN'S
ESSENTIALS
NEW YORK

Published in the United States by St. Martin's Essentials, an imprint of
St. Martin's Publishing Group

THE WAY OF THE FEARLESS WRITER. Copyright © 2022 by Beth Kempton. All
rights reserved. Printed in the United States of America. For information, address
St. Martin's Publishing Group, 120 Broadway, New York, NY 10271.

www.stmartins.com

The Library of Congress Cataloging-in-Publication Data
is available upon request.

ISBN 978-1-250-89213-3 (trade paperback)
ISBN 978-1-250-89214-0 (ebook)

Our books may be purchased in bulk for promotional, educational, or business
use. Please contact your local bookseller or the Macmillan Corporate and
Premium Sales Department at 1-800-221-7945, extension 5442, or by email
at MacmillanSpecialMarkets@macmillan.com.

Originally published in 2022 in the United Kingdom by Piatkus

First U.S. Edition: 2023

10 9 8 7 6 5 4 3 2 1

This book is dedicated to
the spirit of writing
and all who dance with her

gazing at the moon

face reflected in the glass

a blank page awaits

A Note on the Exercises in This Book

I know from experience as a writer and mentor that a lot of us don't know how to begin. Or keep going. Or finish a piece. I promise you, it's totally normal. Luckily, writing exercises can help.

Sometimes all it takes is to say, "Tell me about ..." and set yourself a timer for five minutes, ten minutes, half an hour. Tell me about your grandmother. Tell me about apples. Tell me about the last time you got hurt. Pick a topic—off you go. But when we set our own exercises, our biases and tendencies are already at work, so getting writing exercises from other places can really help. In this book there are fifty writing exercises for you to try. As you write, it's quite possible that these exercises will open the floodgates for all sorts of things to come up and spill out. That is absolutely okay. In fact, it's welcome. But it's really important that you take responsibility for your own self-care in this process. Find some support and seek professional help if you need it. Allow whatever wants to come up to come up, but be gentle on yourself as you write it down.

I encourage you to try every exercise at least once. Spend as little or as much time as you like. Use a timer, or don't. It's up to you. I encourage you to write without editing as you go, to get into the habit of writing down whatever wants to be written without censoring between brain and page.

You can repeat any exercise on a different day, in a different season, or at a different life stage, or relate it to a new project, and you will get something different every time. You can follow all the exercises in the book with a writing group, or you can take the book on retreat and binge several exercises in a day. You could combine two or more exercises to birth a hybrid one of your own. It's up to you.

I encourage you to start a new notebook so that you can look back at the end and see how far you have traveled. Take your writing seriously, but don't be too serious. Write something funny from time to time. Have fun. I have no doubt that there will be times when you are staggered by the depth and beauty of the words you produce. Let's not perpetuate the myth that all writing is hard and painful. It's often a joyful, liberating experience. I hope these exercises will help you to connect with the sense of freedom that writing can bring.

Okay, it's time to write. Come as you are and let things flow.

PS: Whenever you share work that has come from one of these exercises, feel free to tag me @bethkempton #fearlesswriter. I'd love to see what you write.

Contents

Part Two: Initiation

Part Three: Integration

Prologue

The taxi driver pulled up suddenly, jabbing his finger toward a side street and indicating that this was as far as my ride would go. I handed over a 20 *yuán* note and stepped out into a downpour. By the time he had screeched off, rain was needling its way along my spine, my hair was stuck to my face, and I was questioning my decision to meet up with colleagues from the China office in some random Beijing bar.

The side street was all silver and black, moonlight reflected in rippling puddles as far as I could see. There was no sign of any nightlife, but the driver had been clear that it was down this way. A crack of thunder urged me on through the rain, following the narrow road around a bend. Wearing glasses made it harder to see, but I could make out an orange glow up ahead. Shoulders hunched against the weather, I hurried toward it and burst in, expecting excitable chatter, music perhaps. But as the door closed behind me muffling the storm outside, a bell tinkled—and then silence.

I removed my glasses, wiped them on my trouser leg, and put them back on as my eyes adjusted to the light. I took in a man behind a counter in the corner who nodded and went back to his book. None of the usual *"huānyíng guānglín"* to welcome a new customer.

This was not a bar. It was a bookshop. But not a bookshop like any bookshop I had ever been in. It was tiny, with shelves and shelves of leather-bound old books in shades of brown and red. There was something odd about it, but I wasn't quite sure what.

A head popped out from behind the tall stack at the back and said, in a Canadian accent, "Have you read the *Dáodéjīng*?" "Sorry?" I replied, apologizing in the form of a question in the way we do when we're nervous. I had an undergraduate degree from the Department of East Asian Studies at a good British uni-versity, and a masters from another. I had a copy of the *Dáodéjīng* back home, having been inspired to buy it years ago after a late-night drunken conversation on the meaning of life. But East Asian Studies was vast, and I had majored in Japanese, which had taken up a lot of headspace, so this most important of ancient Chinese texts had languished on the shelf.

While I was searching my brain for the details of the teaching and wondering why the stranger behind the bookshelf was asking me about it, he glanced over to the shopkeeper and said something in rapid Mandarin. They both looked at me, then looked back at each other half-laughing, not unkindly, more out of pity. The shopkeeper shrugged and went back to his book.

"Hmm . . ." the Canadian man murmured, and wandered over to another bookshelf. As he traced his way along the spines, I real-ized that none of them had titles. That's why the place felt so weird. His finger stopped at a small brown volume, not much bigger than my hand and about an inch thick. He pulled it off the shelf and handed it to me. "The *Dáodéjīng*," he said. "I think you'd like it."

I put my handbag down, conscious of the rain dripping off the hem of my coat and spreading into small patches on the floor. I stepped toward the man and took the book in both hands. It was soft to the touch, tied with a shoelace of leather. *I'll open it backward then they'll know I'm not just a tourist*, I thought, hoping to claw back a bit of respect for knowing that old Chinese books, like traditional Japanese books, work in reverse, starting at what a Westerner like me might know as the back. The text is written and read from top to bottom, with the lines of characters stacked vertically right to left. Ready to impress, I flipped the book over, held it in my left palm, and carefully opened the cover. But the inside was blank. Every single page was empty.

I looked to the others for an explanation—a copy of the *Dáodéjīng* should be full of profound ideas, not blank pages—but before I could say anything, the Canadian guy, who was now standing by the shop entrance, started quoting Confucius. "When a friend comes from afar, is it not indeed a pleasure?" Then he called a greeting over his shoulder, held his coat above his head, and disappeared into the wet black night.

The bell tinkled once more. Still the shopkeeper said nothing. Confused, I picked up a book from the display table in front of me and flicked through the pages. Nothing there either. I went from shelf to shelf, pulling books down, but to no avail. It felt like some kind of Zen *kōan*: a doorway to some important truth. But all the words were missing.

From One Writer to Another

Oh hello there, do come in.

I may look like I'm just sitting here, pen in hand scribbling in my notebook, but I'm not. I am actually perched with my feet on the moon, watching the world at play beneath me. Did you know I can make those people fall in love and those people fight? Oh yes. I can give that man courage and that child a new friend. I can despair at the state of the world, or try to make sense of it. I can reach into the hearts of other people and make them feel less alone.

Now I am flying across time zones and centuries, guided by the wind, my way lit by the stars. I am woman, I am bird. I am the wild shadow of sorrow and the fragrant flower of life. I am hope, I am memory. I am time itself.

Maybe later today I will carve poetry into the riven bark of the weeping willow in the garden of my childhood home. I might go to the shore, smash my hurt on the rocks, and watch my tears become the ocean. Perhaps I will sleep in the forest and wake to a world of talking animals. I might gather with others around a fire telling stories of seeds and bones buried deep—or fill ancient caves with laughter and song. Or I might just be here, quietly at my desk, sipping tea, waiting for the sun to rise.

This is the writing life.

Sounds pretty special, right? It can be. But before you cast this book aside thinking that it's all right for me but you have family obligations, an exhausting job, and self-doubt you wear strung around your neck like a favorite scarf, let me tell you a few things about myself. I didn't have a book published until the year I turned forty. I have two small children and run my own business, and I have carried so much self-doubt that I'm still amazed that my words have made it to the printed page. Until my first book, *Freedom Seeker*, came out, my work kept me behind the scenes, and I was wholly unsure about stepping in front of the curtain to share personal stories with the world. But the book demanded to be written, so I had to find a way.

It has taken me several years to realize that it wasn't just a way, it was a Way: the Way of the Fearless Writer. And I want to share it with you, because it changed my writing life, and it might just change yours.

Why write?

To write is to pay attention to your life and to open up the channel for magic and mystery to flow through you. When I use the word "writing" in this book, I mean any kind of utterance of words onto the page, including short stories, random musings, entire novels, works of nonfiction, poetry, social media posts, magazine articles, plays, academic work, screenwriting, memoir, even personal correspondence.

We tend to put writing into categories, but writing is about so much more than putting words on paper in a certain format or with a particular purpose. It's about listening. It's about opening. And it's about accessing what lives below the surface so that the ink spills beauty, insights, stories, and truth. Even the most formal of writing can be transformed into a powerful, compelling piece by a fearless writer.

Writing can be medicine for our modern ills. It can be a tool to help us excavate our lives and begin to understand ourselves and others. It can help us grapple with desire, navigate change, cope with stress, celebrate, offer thanks, grieve, heal, and inspire others. Writing can be a means of escape, or a way to arrive fully in this moment, appreciating the miracle of life in the smallest details. And, let's not forget, it can be a pleasure too. But writing cannot be or do any of these things if fear gets in the way and the writer does not write.

An invitation

I invite you to embark on a sacred journey with me, a pilgrimage along an old road: the wild and beautiful path of the fearless writer. If you accept, there is no turning back. You will discover that being a fearless writer has little to do with validation and accolades as we are conditioned to believe. Rather, it is about ritual, dedication, and commitment, developing an acute awareness of beauty, dancing with inspiration, listening to the world outside yourself, and going deep within.

In a radical departure from standard advice about creative success, which involves painful effort, the pursuit of perfection, and the tyranny of critique, this book will show you that there is another way to thrive: a path of ease, discovery, and wonder.

Along the way you will learn how to free your mind so that your body can create, transform your relationship with fear, and write any time, anywhere. You will also notice a growing eagerness to share your work with others, however unlikely that might seem right now, and you'll experience the joy of shining your light for them.

In theory it has never been easier to share your words, but in reality it has probably never been harder. The smart technology, self-publishing tools, and social media platforms that now make it possible to distribute your words instantly and reach people anywhere, have also bred unprecedented competition, a culture of unsolicited feedback, and the curse of comparison at every turn. Add to this the daily pressures of our busy lives and constant media noise, and it's no wonder that those of us who long to write find ourselves stumbling and stalling, or simply not writing at all.

Discovering the path

I have been writing for as long as I can remember, but I did not become a fearless writer until the age of thirty-nine when I was cracked wide open by an extraordinary experience that I will share later in the book. Before that I was plagued by fear and self-doubt, like many writers. It was so bad it almost stopped me finishing *Freedom Seeker*. In fact, it was so bad it nearly stopped me starting. The fear manifested as obsessive perfectionism and a need for control. The more I tried, the harder it got. Until it all got too much, and I finally surrendered. That's when the whole book came flooding out.

Just a few months later I began working on *Wabi Sabi*, which took me back to my second home of Japan, and deep into my academic roots of Japanese language, culture, and philosophy. The more I researched, traveled, interviewed, listened, and wrote, the more I understood that so much of what I would pour into *Wabi Sabi*—particularly ideas about acceptance, impermanence, and dealing with failure—were as true for writing as they were for life.

I got curious about the role of energy, movement, and meditation in my own writing practice, and I trained as a *Reiki* Master and a yoga teacher, not so that I could offer paid treatments or teach classes, but rather to unravel the connections between mind, body, spirit, breath, and words.

All through this I carried on writing—first *Wabi Sabi*, then *Calm Christmas* and *We Are in This Together*—I watched in astonishment as my books were translated into more than twenty-five languages and sold all over the world.

Something had shifted. I had a sense that I had assimilated my lifelong curiosity about Eastern ideas into my writing practice, but I couldn't yet articulate quite how.

I had an emerging theory though, and I started to test it out as I guided more than twenty thousand people through online writing sanctuaries and live writing hours, and led seasonal poetry challenges for my Instagram community, inspiring millions of words, including many from people who hadn't written since school.

Intrigued, I went back to my philosophy texts, cultural commentaries, anthologies of ancient poetry and literature, and more than one hundred of my own journals. I searched for parallels between Eastern ideas about the way the world works and the development of my own writing practice. I traced the evolution of each of my books, paying particular attention to how I had dealt with the myriad fears that arose as I worked on each manuscript. I was hoping to find a clue or two that might help me understand what had changed. What I actually discovered was so much more: there were footprints and a path.

The three sacred gates

I looked at the before and after of my experience of surrender to see what had changed. This is what I was doing before, based on my education and Western societal conditioning:

I was focused on my own desire I had a fixed vision of what I wanted for that first book (for it to be a bestseller), which was putting a huge amount of pressure on me as a first-time author. Although I absolutely wanted the book to inspire people, I am embarrassed to say that my true ambition was related to what the book would do for me and my career. Because my reputation was so caught up with this goal, I was also trying to control what the book would become and how it would be received by the world.

I was obsessed with form I wanted to write the perfect book. Nothing less would do. I had a naive view that I would begin at page one and write until it was done, and I got frustrated when the sentences I tried to write did not flow as I had expected. I was trying to control the quality of my paragraphs and pages without giving them time to breathe. I was also trying to nail down my idea too soon, based on a fixed notion of what it should be.

I was hostage to the idea of our separateness I thought that everyone else was judge, critic, and competition, so I refused to ask anyone for help and got sidetracked by what other authors were doing.

None of it worked, and in a moment of desperation that you'll read about later, I gave up on all of it. Not on the idea of writing, but on the idea of how writing should be. From then on I approached writing *Freedom Seeker* like this:

I let go of my own desire, relinquishing any specific ambitions for the book, and I simply focused on the practice of writing instead. I started to treat that practice as sacred. I brought ritual to my work and opened up to not knowing what would happen next. I entertained the paradox that our writing matters immensely, and not at all. In doing so **I experienced the freedom of embracing DESIRELESSNESS.**

I wrote what wanted to be written, putting it on the page without judgment. I learned that editing was a separate process that I could engage with once I had done the deep work and surfaced the truth of what needed to be said. I abandoned all attempts to force my idea too soon, instead giving it time to be floaty and undefined for a while before gently coaxing it into a shape that would eventually become the book. **I realized that there was value in FORMLESSNESS as well as form.**

An extraordinary encounter with the natural world at that moment of surrender reminded me of the interconnectedness of everything. I stopped seeing everyone else as judge, critic, and competition, and I proactively started building a network of supportive writers and mentors. I also spent more of my writing time in nature, sensing how we are part of something much bigger than us, and **I was reminded of the Buddhist concept of EMPTINESS.** Soon after this my research for *Wabi Sabi* made me think deeply about the notion of impermanence, and how everything arises and dissipates in time, a truth integral to that idea of emptiness.

It was only when I was out walking one day that I realized the significance of all of this. Without realizing it I had metaphorically passed through three sacred gates collectively known in Buddhism as the Three Gates of Liberation: *Muganmon* (無願門) The Gate of Desirelessness, *Musōmon* (無相門) The Gate of Formlessness, and *Kūmon* (空門) The Gate of Emptiness.

With each gate my writing deepened, I found more courage to share my words, and I became more familiar to myself. I was discovering a completely new approach to writing, one where fear does not get in the way.

With the benefit of hindsight I can see how the path of pilgrimage I have walked—from self-conscious secretive writer to grateful published author—has allowed me to shed my conditioning and pass through these three sacred gates. I have written myself free. And now, five books later, here I am at my writing desk, sipping tea, talking to you, and waiting for the sun to rise.

I believe that a flourishing writing life is waiting for you too. This book will guide you through those sacred gates toward it.

In Japan, gates are as symbolic as they are practical. Temple and shrine gates signify a passage from the mundane everyday world outside the gate to the sacred space within. This book is divided into three parts—Invitation, Initiation, and Integration—representing the three stages of your journey toward becoming a fearless writer. Each part leads you toward one of the gates, which you must pass through to continue on to the next part of the journey. As we cross the threshold of each gate we will release what we no longer need, and we will grow in confidence as fearless writers.

Each part of the book begins with a Journey Note: a contemplative essay offering a principle for you to carry with you on that section of the journey. I have taken inspiration from the Japanese essay style known as *zuihitsu*, which means "writing freely without any particular structure or form." A free-flowing stream of loosely connected ideas, observations, and musings. A following of the ink-wet brush. I have chosen this style to reflect, as closely as possible, the way my mind works when I am writing. That is a risk, because my writing mind does not work in a logical way. It meanders from memory to meditation, from a fragment of philosophy to the glimpse of a dream. But I want you to see this so that you know that when your writing mind does the same, it's okay. It's safe. It will lead you somewhere.

You will see from each Journey Note that ideas pour in from all over, swirl around each other, merge together, and flow toward some vast place just out of view, the way that a river leads to the sea. I hope you will read these essays with an open mind, following the thought trail, not grasping for exact definitions, but allowing the words to wash over you, spilling your own ideas into the river, and drinking all you need.

Each essay is followed by four practical chapters, which serve as the four steps up toward the next gate. Each chapter offers a host of honest stories from my own writing life along with writing exercises for you to try, so by the time you arrive at the next gate you will be ready to pass through it and proceed to the next stage of the path.

I am sharing this with you not as a guru who has reached the end of the path, but as a fellow pilgrim still walking it—always walking it—simply reaching back and offering a friendly guiding hand as you join me on the path so that we can walk it together.

I encourage you to read the book from start to finish, in order, so that you don't miss anything, ideally completing each writing exercise as you go. I hope that you will then keep the book on your writing desk to dip into for reminders and inspiration at any time.

Although *The Way of the Fearless Writer* is inspired by ideas from Japan and China, this book is not an in-depth guide to any particular aspect of philosophy, religion or history. Rather, it is a radical approach to writing (and care of the writer) informed by over two decades of exposure to Japanese ideas, culture, and language, some of which have distant roots in China. Some of those ideas are too complex to investigate fully in a book about writing, and I offer them here simply as invitations. I encourage you to contemplate each offering as a portal to your own vault of wisdom.

So, my friend, the time has come. Take a deep breath and open your heart to the mystery. May the sacred journey begin.

BONUS CONTENT

To help you on your way, I have prepared some special bonus content for you, which you can find online at bethkempton.com/fearlesswriter. This includes a meditation album and *The Fearless Writer's Toolkit*, a package of resources to support you on your journey. Help yourself!

Part One
Invitation

The First Gate: *Muganmon*

無願門

The Gate of Desirelessness

To approach *Muganmon*, the Gate of Desirelessness, we need to:

- Learn to write any time, anywhere, without trying to control what spills out.
- Choose to serve the writing, not the ego.
- Learn how to use our awareness to dissolve attachments and breathe life into our words.

Only then can we pass through the first gate and accept fearlessly that we are writers without attaching to a certain way of being as a writer.

Journey Note 1

Toward the Gate of Desirelessness

In the West, our tendency seems to be to work hard, push for results, and bulldoze our way through anything difficult—or try to bury it instead. The classic Chinese text known as the *Dáodéjīng* offers different counsel. *Dáo* (sometimes *tao*), written 道, means "way" or "path" and describes both the essential, unnameable process of the universe and the path of life. In Japanese this character is read *dō* and is used in martial arts and cultural practices to describe a school or discipline, such as 空手道 (*karatedō*) karate, or The Way of the Empty Hand, and 書道 (*shodō*) calligraphy, or The Way of Writing. The character 道 can also be read *michi* in Japanese, in which case it means "road."

The *Dáodéjīng* (sometimes written *Tao Te Ching* and often referred to as *The Book of the Way*), is a poetic and powerful compilation of wisdom, which has become the most translated of all philosophical work in Chinese. Dating back over two thousand years, it is traditionally attributed to a figure known as Laozi (sometimes written Lao Tzu), although it is likely to have had a long gestation in different hands. Its mystical nature has generated a host of interpretations, but all center on the notion of *wú wéi*, conventionally translated from the Chinese as "nonaction." This is not passivity, but rather letting things take their natural course, embracing spontaneity, and not trying to control things. It means having your mind perfectly attuned to an activity or situation so that no conscious effort is needed to accomplish it.

There are also frequent references to the natural world, reminding us that birds are not always in flight and the skies do not always storm. In some ways it is an ode to *zìrán*, the Chinese term for naturalness, or embracing things as they are. The *Dáodéjīng* also emphasizes *de* which translates from the Chinese as "power" or "virtue," not in the moral sense but rather as a property inherent in something. This is sometimes described as "authenticity" or "skill at living."

This is the wisdom of listening, practicing, and trusting without trying to force outcomes. In recent years I have discovered that this is also the wisdom of fearless writing.

This approach is not easy for anyone brought up in a results-driven society. We want to be famous already. We want assurances that what we write will be good so that we don't waste our time. We want perfect sentences to come out and we get frustrated when they don't. We have a fixed idea about what kind of writer we should be and what we should write about, and we hold tightly to that. But what if we could see that in doing all this we are fighting against the current when we could just as easily flow with it? What if, instead, we simply follow our curiosity and intuition, and go wherever our hearts want to go?

I wish I had considered this before I wrote my first book. It would have saved me a whole lot of pain. It began, as many stories do, with a meltdown on my bedroom floor. I was a heavily pregnant workaholic small-business owner with a toddler and a head full of noise. That particular day I was supposed to go to London to talk on a panel about whether "do what you love" was good advice. As the founder of a company called Do What You Love, you can imagine which side of the argument I was on, except that I was stressed and exhausted, and not a great advertisement for what I believed in. I was regretting accepting the invitation. And then I went to get dressed and couldn't do up my jeans. It's the mouse that sinks the boat.

As I lay on the floor, staring at the ceiling wondering what had happened to my life, I had a flashback of riding up a mountain path on horseback to Paro Taktsang, the Tiger's Nest monastery, after a surprise dinner with the Prince of Bhutan. It felt like a dream, so far was that moment from my daily life now. I watched myself standing alone, inhaling silence at the edge of the mountain as a gentle mist tumbled over the rice paddies of the Paro Valley three thousand feet below.

The flashback was enough to make me see that I had once known freedom, but in recent years I had trapped myself by chasing a specific and unhealthy idea of success. I dragged myself up from the bedroom floor and went outside to stand barefoot in a patch of afternoon sun. As I breathed deeply, I felt a space open up in my heart.

I went back indoors and rummaged in my desk for a notebook, determined to start journaling again. Emptying my head onto its pages over the next few weeks brought some clarity, and I booked five months off for maternity leave.

My sweet baby arrived in July, and I spent the summer carrying her up and down Brighton seafront pondering what it takes to feel free. It felt like a big enough question for a book. I decided to put a proposal together and things moved faster than I expected. I landed an agent and a book deal before returning to work. But that's when the trouble began. I spent far too long fiddling around with the structure of the book on an Excel spreadsheet, moving chapters back and forth, switching the location of ideas, and re-naming sections without actually writing anything. One day, a few months in, Mr. K glanced at my laptop screen and hastily rearranged his furrowed brow. "Are you still working on that? Shouldn't you be writing something by now?" I was devastated. He had found me out. I had no idea how to write a book. I was terrified of the whole project. I was scared of sharing my stories, but even more than that, I was scared of the fact that I had no idea how to get those stories out of my head and onto the page. "I give up. It isn't working. I need a miracle to get this done."

Mr. K looked at me and said, "I think you need to get away for a while." Before I could protest about the time or the expense, he had booked me on a flight to Costa Rica. I traveled to Nosara via an old friend's sea-fishing lodge in Paquera. By the time I arrived at the hotel I was still clueless about how I was going to get the book written, but I was beginning to trust that it would work out. I had surrendered all notions of trying to control what the book would become, or how my career would take shape as a result. I was just there, ready to write, waiting to see.

At breakfast the duty manager sat down next to me and said, "The strangest thing has happened. Those people over there are leaving today, and we have had a string of cancelations. You are going to have the whole place to yourself for the rest of the week. Why don't we put a table in the middle of the yoga rancho so that you can see the ocean as you write?"

They brought me Costa Rican coffee and put fresh flowers on the table, and I danced with howler monkeys as Xavier Rudd's "Follow the Sun" rolled across the jungle. Pretty amazing, right? But that wasn't the miracle. As sunset approached the hotel staff moved my desk to the side of the rancho to make space for their regular kundalini yoga class, held for locals. Joining in, I rolled out my mat, unaware that I was about to have an experience that would change my writing life.

The circular rancho had a vast conical roof, held up by individual tree trunks that framed the jungle beyond. Hummingbirds were flitting through the trees. In the class we were doing a simple pose, our hands pressed together above our heads, first fingers pointing upward. "Reach for your life," called our teacher, Angie, unaware of the potency of her words. As I stretched up I felt myself crack open. Out of the corner of my eye I sensed something moving. A bird of prey was flying over the Pacific, now swooping, now soaring. The black hawk-eagle spread her wings further, catching the soft breeze and gliding over the jungle. She moved closer, silhouetted against the setting sun.

I changed pose and looked up to see the huge bird heading straight for us. At the last possible moment she swooshed right past the yoga shala, and in that second I was electrified, as if her spirit had leaped from her body right into my soul. For a split second everything went white. Fire shot up my spine and tears streamed down my face. And then I knew. The formlessness of freedom had taken the form of the bird, which transferred a formless sense of freedom into me, soon to shape-shift once more into the form of words on the page. Having written nothing for four months, I wrote thirty thousand words in the next four days, and I haven't stopped writing since.

That eagle encounter became the moment after which everything about my writing life was different.

I happened to have this experience a few thousand miles from home, but I promise that you don't need to get on a plane to see the great mystery of this world. You just have to open your mind and heart, and your notebook—and write.

*

I used to take a logical approach to everything. I believed that if I made a plan, followed the steps, and worked hard, I'd get where I wanted to go. But writing doesn't work like that. Of course, there are practical things that we can do to get started and keep going. We can create conditions conducive to writing, embrace ritual, and actively seek inspiration. We can commit time, keep showing up, hone our craft, and shape our words with care. We can choose what we want to write today: a short story, a poem, a scene perhaps. It can be helpful to know roughly what we are trying to create, because that affects the way we approach it.

But somewhere between the inputs and the outputs we can influence there is a kind of mysterious alchemy that happens, and to suggest that we are in charge of that would be to give ourselves too much credit. This is where trust comes in. And trust means being open to what might happen, without trying to force a particular result.

An obsession with results in the outer world is damaging to our work in the inner world. But without the inner work, there is no hope of any kind of lasting external "success" anyway. That is why we begin our journey walking in the direction of *Muganmon* (無願門), the Gate of Desirelessness. 門 is the character for gate, and the characters used for the name of this gate mean "no" or "without" (無) and "desire," "wish" or "aim" (願). Some people refer to it as "aimlessness," others as "no goals." I must confess that having been raised to avoid laziness at all costs, intellectually I find this notion challenging, because I associate it with a lack of ambition. Goals help me to prioritize and organize my life. They give me a sense of direction, even if I know deep down that I have no idea what tomorrow will bring. But emotionally I am all in. Life is the moment-to-moment unfolding of the world, which ironically we so often miss in our relentless pursuit of success. Through writing I have realized that instead of focusing on a singular material goal in the hope of a return in the future, my life is richer if I dedicate myself to the act of writing, right here in the present.

This obsession with what we want to have happen in the future, and our race to get there at the expense of what is happening now, is not a recent development for humanity, as Yoshida Kenkō shared in his *Tsurezuregusa* (*Essays in Idleness*) back in the 14th century:

> We may not be aware of the passing instants, but as we go on ceaselessly spending them, suddenly the term of life is upon us. For this reason, the man who practices the Way should not begrudge the passage of distant time to come, but the wasting of a single present moment.[1]

It is so true, but even as I write this, I can feel the resistance. What's wrong with a goal of writing a bestseller, for example? Well, nothing, if that helps you carve out time for writing—but know that whether or not it happens in the way you expect is out of your control. A very specific succeed-or-fail high-stakes ego-based goal also brings with it all kinds of energetic baggage. It's much easier if you simply decide to write it, and then dedicate yourself to doing your best today, instead of wasting precious time and energy wondering whether anyone will like it tomorrow.

It was only once I let go of the need to control the outcome of doing the work that I was able to start writing my first book. Letting go of my own desire led me to create something that could serve others, and in the long run supported my writing life too, in ways I had not even imagined.

To write in service of the writing, not the ego, is a radical act. What if we gathered up all the energy we usually spend worrying about what other people think and poured it into our writing? What if we really lived our lives, moment to moment, and wrote about that? What if we wrote to release what is burning inside us, allowing that to be enough for now?

When we do this we realize that everything we need is already here. We do not need any kind of external validation or material success in order to write, or keep writing. When we focus on writing as a sacred act, we stop trying to control what happens. A writing life stops being something we dream about and becomes something we are already living. But it's not enough for me to tell you this. You must learn to inhabit such a truth for yourself. This is the path we must walk to reach the first gate on our sacred journey.

As we prepare for this adventure, questions begin to bubble up. How will we get ourselves to the desk to begin when we have so many demands on our time? How will we find the energy to be creative when life is so exhausting? How will we decide what to write about when we are feeling uninspired? How will we break through writer's block, if it appears? How on earth will we manage to silence the mind chatter long enough to write? The answer to all of these questions lies with a small but powerful word: *ki*.

The character 気 (*ki*) is defined in a leading Japanese character dictionary as "vital energy, spirit, breath of life, vitality."[2] In martial arts traditions, *ki* represents a source of spiritual strength, and in Japan it is used philosophically to refer to a function of life that flows throughout the universe and through each one of us.[3] We can cultivate it and develop a stronger sense of vitality and dynamism, or allow it to drain out, leaving us feeling sluggish and stagnant. *Ki* is the key to inspired, fearless writing.

Inspired = with breath, alive.
Uninspired = lacking breath, lifeless.

From a young age we are taught that writing comes from our heads. Think of something to say. Write it down. Sit still. Don't fidget. Use nice, controlled handwriting. Check for grammar and spelling mistakes. I get it. These are the fundamentals we build from, and the discipline is useful. But it's missing half the story: the wild half.

We sense the world with our animal body. We store our experiences—the joy, the pain, the secrets—within that body. They crackle beneath the skin, imprint themselves onto the face, and speak through body language. The retrieval of images, in the form of memories or imagined scenes, can be a tangible experience beyond scratching words onto paper with a pen. The act of writing can make us cry or laugh, feel dizzy or tense, elated or in physical pain. But no one tells us about this. No one tells us that this is okay or normal. And no one tells us that it is actually the key to deeper writing and to the elimination of writer's block.

When we engage with our breath and our bodies *before we write* and *as we write*, the experience of writing is elevated. We can retreat from the chatter of busy mind and reach into the depths of wild mind, shifting our stuck energy and transmitting a sense of aliveness into our words.

The breath of the world flows through you.
Don't let it stagnate.
Inhale.
Be still.
Exhale.
Be still.

Keep on breathing.
Keep on writing.
That's all you have to do.
Flowing in rhythm, in sync with life itself.

Over the next four chapters you will learn how to quieten the noise in your life so that you can bring your full attention to writing, bring ritual to your practice, release any blocks, cultivate *ki,* and pour energy into your words without concern for what might happen next.

By the time you reach the Gate of Desirelessness you will be ready to accept your identity as a writer fearlessly, while detaching from any specific idea about what kind of a writer you are or should be. Are you ready?

Chapter 1

QUIETENING

隗より始めよ
(kai yori hajimeyo)

When embarking on a great
project, start where you are with
something small.

JAPANESE PROVERB

"A thousand-mile journey begins with a single step."[1] So says the *Dáodéjīng*, collated more than two thousand years ago by the sage Laozi (sometimes referred to as Lao Tzu). It also says, "Confront the difficult while it is still easy."[2]

However great our ambitions for writing, let's start small, with a single word. Any word will do. Scribble it right there in the margin, or open a new notebook and write it on the first page. One word. That's all. Just sit with that word for a moment. Ponder why that particular word came to you. Write a bit about that, if you like. Now you have started, here's a question for you: as we set out on this pilgrimage together, what is your intention? Write that down too.

We often make a huge deal of starting. We make all sorts of excuses. Maybe it'll be easier to concentrate when the children are in bed. Maybe tomorrow we'll have a clearer head. Maybe next month we'll get a new job so we have Mondays to write. Yes maybe, but don't spend today wondering about the maybes. Spend today writing. Always spend today writing, and before you know it you'll be living a writing life, and the maybes will have taken care of themselves.

It's really not that complicated. We simply need to choose to begin.

If I'm stuck, I will often write "Today" on my page, and then capture a few precious fragments.

Today. Small hands baking gingerbread hearts. Gray streaks in my hair. White streaks in the sky. A family of ducks on the lawn. Lettuces popping. Ferns unfurling. A poem about wonder and a pocket full of pennies.

There, a few words on the page, and I have begun. Try it yourself. Doing this regularly makes it easier to begin every time you show up.

Writing any time, anywhere

There is a common thread woven through my favorite poems and passages from long-ago Japan. They were written by people who actively sought out solitude and silence on the road or in quiet mountain huts, such as poet and Zen Master Ryōkan Taigu who lived alone on Mount Kugami two centuries ago. In one beautiful untitled poem he wrote of playing a lute with no string, with a silent melody that entered wind and cloud, mingled with a stream, filled out the dark valley, blew through the vast forest, and then disappeared. Peering into the heart of the human condition he asked, *"Other than those who hear emptiness, / Who will capture this rare sound?"*[3]

Finding space and quiet to ponder life in this way is neither easy nor practical for many of us in the modern world. We have jobs to go to, bills to pay, and families to care for, not to mention a media addiction to attend to. But those are just logistics to deal with, not reasons not to write.

Solitude is fertile. We need to find ways to step away from the noise and enter a sacred writing space. We need a hermitage of our own: a humble, empty room with a crack in the roof where the moon shines through. In this hermitage we can write without distraction and reach through what is in front of us to discover what lies beyond.

The grandest version of this might be a separate physical place to retreat to, set days of the week dedicated to writing, or time away somewhere peaceful. If those things are possible for you, by all means embrace them, but don't let them become prerequisites for writing.

> A sacred writing space does not have to be a physical place. It can be a state of the heart that you enter through ritual and silence.

When you wake in the night and the world is still, pay attention. When the wind shows its presence by rustling leaves, pay attention. When you take a slow deep breath and feel the beating of your own heart, pay attention. These quiet moments are secret ways in.

My sacred morning ritual looks like this. I wake at 5 a.m. and go downstairs in the dark. I switch on the fairy lights in the kitchen and put the kettle on. While the water is boiling I do a simple movement sequence to loosen up my body. Then I make tea and toast, take it into my study, and close the door behind me. I sit at my desk, where my notebook and pen are waiting, along with a candle and a box of matches. I take a few deep breaths, inhaling the gentle energy of early morning, then I light the candle and welcome a new page.

I write the time, the date, and the place, anchoring myself to the moment, a still point in the rushing river of life. *5:10 a.m. Thursday 16 January. At my desk.* Then I write what I notice. *Still dark. Silver rain is falling from the street lamp. The hot water just clicked on.* Every day is slightly different, depending on the season.

Often I read some poetry, a short passage from a favorite book, or some words of my own. I call this my Daily Spark. It's usually enough to set the words flowing. If I don't feel any words bubbling up, I might meditate on the candle for a while and come up with a question. Then I'll respond to that question in my notebook, and off I go. When you approach writing with this kind of ritual, you never really have a blank page.

The ritual signals that it's time to write. The more you do it, the quicker you'll be able to go deep when you arrive at the page. Just as the ritual of bowing by host and guests begins and ends a traditional Japanese tea ceremony, your writing ritual gives shape to your writing session with a clear opening and closing.

We tend to organize our days as if they are linear, but when you begin a writing session with a ritual, you carve out a circular space off to the side of your day. You leave the day at a given point—and come back to it. A casual observer might think that just a few minutes have passed and nothing special has happened, but you know the truth. For a while you entered a place where time bends, ideas hover, and anything is possible. Every time you step into your own sacred writing space to greet your words you change a little, grow a little. And then, when you are ready, you close the ritual, come back to your day, and carry on, as if you haven't just traveled to other worlds and back.

HOW TO CREATE YOUR OWN SACRED WRITING SPACE

Step one: leave the world behind

- Physically step away from the world (close a door, or go to a café perhaps).
- Switch off your phone and get quiet.

Step two: settle in

- Light a candle, breathe mindfully, do a short meditation or use some other intentional marker to signify that it is time to write.
- Open your notebook or laptop and write the moment onto the page. This might include details such as the date and time, your location, and any sensory observations.

Step three: write

You can simply keep writing, or you can prompt something unexpected in one of the following ways:

- Read or listen to a "spark" (a stimulus such as a poem, passage or a writing exercise). Write a response and carry on from there.
- Pull out an existing piece of writing and go deeper on it.
- Ask a question and let your pen lead you toward an answer.

▶

Step four: prepare to wrap up

- Come to a close with a timer or bell, or at a natural point.
- Be mindful about the last sentence, consciously signing off or marking your place so that you can return easily next time.
- Close your notebook or laptop.
- Take a moment for gratitude.

Step five: return to the world

- Reverse the ritual to close the session (for example, blow out the candle).
- Consciously exit the space and rejoin the world outside.

Have a plan for the next time you are going to return to your sacred writing space. Write it on your calendar. Show up again.

You don't have to roll out the full ritual every time. It's like muscle memory. Once you have done it regularly for a while, there will come a time when recreating even one single aspect of it, like taking out your favorite notebook, will draw you in, ready to write. Sometimes I'm too tired to get up at 5 a.m., so I start later in the day. I skip the toast but make the tea, then I breathe deeply and let the spark lead me in. Sometimes I do a full yoga practice, step outside to gaze at the moon, or go for a long walk, before sitting down to write. It depends on the day, and the season.

I like writing at my desk, but I don't make it a condition of writing. I like lighting a candle first, but I don't make that a condition of writing. I like the rhythm of showing up early before the day begins, but I don't make that a condition of writing either. While routine and a dedicated writing space can encourage you to write, there is value in novelty too. Mixing up where and when you write can bring a potent mix of freshness and serendipity.

Sometimes I sit and write. Sometimes I walk and use my phone to send ideas to myself as they come to me. Inspiration doesn't just arrive obediently when we happen to be sitting at a writing desk. It is at work all the time. Sometimes it comes thundering in, but more often it hovers quietly at the edges of our day and we just can't hear it for the noise. That's why carving out time and space, and honoring your ritual, can really help.

The simplest ritual of all is to breathe mindfully before you write. It centers you, prepares you, and focuses your energy and attention on this writing moment. A few deep breaths can be enough to get the ink flowing, and you can do that any time, anywhere.

WRITE NOW #01

You will need a candle for this exercise, but if you don't have one, simply use your imagination. Sit comfortably, spine tall. Light the candle, rest your hands in your lap, and just watch the flame for ten slow breaths. Now put your hands on your belly and imagine a ball of light and heat behind your palms. Keep breathing slowly, imagining you are drawing the fire from the candle into your body to intensify the fire in your belly. Stay here for a few minutes and let the power of this visualization fill you. Then pick up your pen and write whatever wants to be written.

Find the time to write

If you are struggling to find time to write, it may be because you aren't clear on *why* you want to write. Take a moment to think about that. Having only ever known writing books with small children in my life, my greatest hindrance to putting in the time needed has always been parental guilt. For a long time I couldn't sit down without the voice in my head insisting that I should be with my family, instead of closing the door on them and spending an hour with my ideas.

When I thought about why I write, I came up with many reasons. I do it because it is how I make sense of the world. I do it because it makes me feel connected in a profound way. I do it because it feels good. But perhaps most significantly, I am a better, more awake version of myself for having written. I feel recharged, and I have more patience, compassion, and enthusiasm for everything and everyone else once I have written.

Realizing that writing can be good for me and for my family has really helped me to deal with guilt and get to the page.

Even if you never share your words with anyone else, your writing is not just for you. The positive impact writing can have on your spirit and outlook will benefit your loved ones too. Just this morning my six-year-old asked to borrow my stapler so that she could make her own book, "To be like you, Mummy."

I'll say it again: I am a better version of myself for having written. You might be too.

Sometimes life happens and genuine emergencies keep us from the page. Mostly though, it's just a choice as to whether or not we arrive there. If you are struggling to find time to write, make a list of everything you are finding time to do instead, and start making different choices. Stop ironing. Quit bingeing box sets.

Batch-cook dinners. Get up earlier. We can all find a pocket of quiet somewhere: during the baby's nap, on a tea break, or at the bedside of a cared-for loved one. I challenge you to find a pocket of time to write every day for seven days in a row and see how much easier it becomes.

When you're not choosing writing, why is that? What message are you sending yourself and your family? Ponder this for a while, and then pick up your pen.

WRITE NOW #02

Empty your pockets or your bag for me. Show me what you carry. Tell me a story about that.

Find the energy to write

When I was seven my parents signed me up for *jūdō*. It was my first exposure to anything Japanese. I remember standing barefoot on the mat in the *dōjō* (the practice hall) fiddling with my new white outfit and wondering how on earth I was going to fight the huge teenagers further along the line.

I found out soon enough, when we were taught how to throw using our own balance, concentration, and flow of movement, combined with our opponent's own body weight. My favorite throw was *tai otoshi* (体落とし) which means "body drop." We had to grip our opponent's lapel with one hand and their sleeve with the other, then break their balance by twisting the lapel and pulling on the sleeve. A right foot toward them, and a circling of the left foot round behind us would position us to their side. Then, right leg out, flowing body twist, gravity assists, teenager on the floor. I was astonished every time my small body managed it.

I loved being encouraged to utter a *kiai* (気合), which for me sounded something like "*hyā!*" This spirited shout from the belly is an audible release of stored energy which can intimidate an opponent. It made me feel stronger and more capable as I focused my breath and attention into this single sound and let it fly out of my body.

Jūdō (柔道) literally means "yielding path" and is often described as "the way of gentleness." It is built on a unifying principle known as *seiryoku zenyō* (精力善用), which advocates the most efficient and effective use of one's spiritual and physical energies to achieve an intended purpose.[4] This can be applied to writing, too. To write we need openness, intuition, and belief as much as we need technique, stamina, and vitality.

We can consciously cultivate these energies to support our writing practice, and we can use our writing practice to tune in to and take care of ourselves in return. We can also pay attention to what is draining our energy in everyday life, and take action to address that.

ELEVEN WAYS TO CULTIVATE AND BALANCE YOUR ENERGY

1. Eat well
2. Sleep well
3. Stay hydrated
4. Practice breath awareness
5. Get lots of fresh air

6. Spend time in nature
7. Do regular movement practices such as yoga, tai chi, and qigong
8. Become aware of rhythm: your own heartbeat, in music, the cycle of the seasons
9. Do things that bring you joy
10. Be conscious of the energy of those you spend time with
11. Be truthful on the page, using it as a release when you need to

When we cultivate our energy—along with our curiosity—away from the page in preparation for our time at the page, we are engaged in vital work preparing the ground for all we are yet to write.

After a writing session we often carry the spirit of our words into our day. Even if we don't consciously think about it, our ideas percolate in the background, and often they will have shape-shifted by the time we sit down to write again. In my experience this happens much more frequently when I spend the time in between nourishing mind, body or spirit in some way.

Let the words go

Writing is both sacred and ordinary if ordinary means part of our day-to-day life, and something that anyone can do without any particular training, or money or experience. Yet when we make it sacred in the simplest of ways, by giving it our full attention, we send ourselves an important message about its place in our lives. But it's the process that's sacred, not the individual words that come out. I think we sometimes confuse the two, holding on to specific sentences, stories, and scenes because we like them, even if they don't fit. Sometimes we get attached because they might make us sound smart, or literary,

> It is in letting go of most of our words that we get to the few that really matter.

or because we are astounded at how they seemed to arrive fully formed, almost channeled, and we are paralyzed by the miracle.

Many words end up being sacrificial: we have to spill the surface ones to get to the good stuff. We can carve away the surplus later. For now, let's relax and hold all the words lightly, not being too attached to what lands on the page. Let's allow writing to be our meditation. Nothing more, nothing less.

WRITE NOW #03

Choose one of the topics below and make a list:

- Things you have lost

- Doors you have walked through

- Ways you have been hungry

- Promises you have kept

- Braveries you have witnessed

When you have finished your list, pick one thing on it and write about that.

The work of the fearless writer

My first book, *Freedom Seeker*, led me to this definition: *freedom is the willingness and ability to choose your path and live as your authentic self.* Since then I have discovered that fearless writing is a form of freedom, which is to say: *fearless writing is the willingness and ability to choose your writing path, and write as your authentic self.*

That authentic self is not the ego-construction that we put out in the world and measure against other people, but the consciousness beneath everything, which speaks through the intelligent heart. In the modern world it can be difficult to access this, but with practice, we can. This doesn't mean that you won't ever have doubts or be afraid, because the ego shows up all the time. But you will never be alone with your heart as your compass and writing as your guide. Fewer fears will arise, you will fear less often, and the intensity of your fear will reduce with practice and experience. If your path opens up new fears, you will know to return to your heart and deal with them too.

> The work of the fearless writer is done step by step, day by day.

WRITE NOW #04

Write about the last dream you can remember. Turn it into a story, or look for a message in it. Then, when you go to bed tonight, put a notepad and pen by your bed. If you wake in the night, scribble on it in the dark. Otherwise, note down a few words on waking. Don't look at your notes for a day or so, and then use them as a spark for new writing.

Show up.
Get quiet.
Write.

Chapter 2

RELEASING

Breath is a bridge between body and mind.

KAZUAKI TANAHASHI[1]

I used to lodge with a laid-back Japanese man whose favorite phrase was 気にしないで (*ki ni shinaide*), which means "Don't worry about it." It only recently struck me that the literal translation of this is "Don't turn it into energy." Yet this is often exactly what we do with worries. We can get so fixated on a fear-based thought that we turn it into stuck energy in the body, where it acts as a creative block that gets in the way of our work.

In this chapter we are going to explore ways to use breath and movement to release energy blocks and get the words flowing. I encourage you to approach this in a playful way. Try reconnecting with your inner child. There is an old Japanese proverb that says 三つ子の魂百まで (*mitsugo no tamashii hyaku made*), which means "A person's character at three years old is their character at one hundred." Think back to what you were like when you were young. What did you love to do? What was fun for you? Try that again.

Any time I ask my children if they want to play something or have a dance party they always say yes. We have journaling club every Monday after school. We cut stuff out of magazines, stamp with our fingers, draw maps and houses, write about our dreams. We are not trying to achieve anything; we are just enjoying time together creating, with snacks. I try to bring this attitude to my work. To be honest, writing is often just me and my words enjoying time together, with snacks.

When you feel that you are stagnating, let movement shake things up.

Music can work wonders for cultivating our sense of play too, encouraging us to shake off any seriousness and feel the beat. We can use music to shift our energy and lift our spirits. Listen to the words, feel the rhythm, and let your body follow it. Loud, quiet, fast or slow. Tune in to another culture's music, or sing your heart out to some old favorites. Stick a blank sheet of paper on the wall and write as you dance.

Whole-body writing

The forest was vibrating. Hulking waves of sound rolled through it, unearthing scents and stories from the ground beneath my feet. In the darkness I felt my way along a path between towering *sugi* trees leading up to Murodani Shrine on the outskirts of a small village an hour north of Kyōto. Following village resident Teruyuki Kuchū, I climbed the shrine steps to a low building pulsating with the rhythm of Japanese *taiko* (drums).

"Welcome to Saturday night in Kanbayashi!" he said.

The drumming stopped. Silence thundered into the void, and every cell in my body boomed. Then it began again, beating the ground like an ancient call for rain.

That night, lying on my thin futon on the *tatami* floor of

an old house in the village, I couldn't sleep. The memory of the drums pulsated in my bones. I did a body scan to still my mind, but that night, instead of finding areas of tension to relax, I found old stories of my life in Japan swimming beneath my skin. The dull ache in my back was an overnight ferry crossing from Ōsaka to Beppu in my teens, sleeping alongside a hundred other passengers on *tatami* mats with just a few beans in my pocket. My right elbow sank heavily into the mattress and I relived clutching the doorframe of a friend's kitchen during an earthquake. An involuntary jerk of my ankle released an image of me stepping into a wooden canoe a friend had hand carved and named after me when I went to live in Tōkyō, and how I had wobbled with the emotion of it and nearly fallen in. My body was alive with stories wanting to be heard. I sat up, switched on the small lamp, and wrote for hours.

We are often told to use all our senses in descriptions. To recreate a scene in a temple garden for example, we might think about the sound of water trickling into the bamboo pipe designed for scaring off deer. We use our minds to imagine what the body senses, but we are rarely taught to use the body's capacity for physical experience to help us write. The drumming woke up something in me that calls every time I come to write a vignette or personal story. I sometimes use my physical body to transport me to the kind of experience I am writing about, and at other times I just awaken my body with stretching, breathwork, yoga, or dance, to call the memory to the surface, free my mind to go deep into the experience, and write from there.

> Moving our bodies before and as we write can bring a whole new dimension to our writing.

*

Physical stimuli like the rhythmic drumming of the *taiko* or other powerful sounds, scents, visual reminders or objects open up a trail of possibilities, inviting us to explore what we might not come up with using the mind alone.

If you have never done anything like this, you might feel a little self-conscious to begin with. That's normal. But remember, as we take a step toward the Gate of Desirelessness we are acting in service of the writing, not the ego. Don't worry about what you look like. Have fun!

WRITE NOW #05

You will need headphones and some music with a drumbeat. Try searching the famous drumming troupe Kodō taiko on YouTube. Don't play the music yet. Then follow these steps:

In your notebook write something about the place where you are right now. Go for five minutes.

Remove your shoes and stand barefoot for a minute or so, with your feet hip distance apart—or feel the connection where you are sitting. Relax your shoulders and hold your arms out to the sides, palms facing forward, opening your heart. Imagine that there are roots growing down from your body into the earth beneath you. As you inhale, draw energy up from the earth. As you exhale, release anything you need to release into the earth, knowing that it will be composted. Stay here for twenty breaths.

Now write more about the place you are in. How did you end up there? What kind of energy does the place have? No judgment, just observation. Write for five minutes.

Put on your headphones and turn on the drumming music. Feel the rhythm penetrating deep into your bones. Move with it if you feel drawn to do that. Imagine being deep in a forest and hearing these sounds traveling through the trees. If you feel like you want to utter a sound, do it. Do this for as long as you like, but for at least five minutes.

Then pick up your notebook once more, still listening to the drumming, and write whatever wants to come out. Go for five minutes.

Turn off the drums and feel the vibration of the silence in your ears. Write again for five more minutes.

Read what you have written. What do you notice?

Writing when it's hard

Recently, I was reading *The Breathing Book* by Donna Farhi, and was struck by her message that breathing is one of the simplest things in the world—we breathe in, and we breathe out—but that does not mean it is easy.[2] It's the same with writing. Moving a pen across a page, or hitting keys on a keyboard is simple, but that does not mean writing itself is easy. When we have had a difficult experience, it can take a huge effort to voice what happened. Writing about it is a powerful way to release its hold on us, but it can be painful to relive every detail. When this is the case, it can help to write just a fragment of memory.

Words heal. Apply liberally.

The physical act of writing itself can have a healing effect. The emotional experience of reading aloud what we have written can be healing too. Treasuring, sharing or burning those words can help to close a wound so that only the scar remains.

Life is hard and beautiful, often at the same time. Writing can help us to reach toward each other, see ourselves in each other, and know that we are not alone.

WRITE NOW #06

Pick a situation that you want to write about that happened in the past, and make ten detailed observations around the edge of the experience without actually writing about the experience. Where were you? What could you hear, see, smell, taste or feel just before or at the time of the experience? What detail might hint at what was going on? For example, the silhouette of the woman in the doorway, the phone dropped and smashed on the kitchen floor.

Craft some of these fragments of memory into a short piece of writing or a poem in the past tense.

Then rewrite it in the present and see how it alters the piece.

Writing the story beyond the story

When we are struggling to write, grounding ourselves can help. This means physically reconnecting with the ground beneath us, and it can be as simple as lying on the floor, or standing barefoot outside, and feeling a connection to the earth.

Personally, I like to get my hands in the soil. If I am ever stuck for something to write about, I just step into the garden to watch and listen. Sometimes I bring an object back to my writing desk, to see where it takes me. Physically holding an object in your hands, studying it, and letting it speak to you, can yield all sorts of ideas. Take this grubby gardening glove, for example. It fell off the shelf as I opened the shed door, and I want to share with you how I might use it as a stimulus for writing.

I put the glove on and notice how some of the dried earth falls off it as I stretch my fingers. The roughness reminds me of the hours we spent building raised beds during the pandemic. That leads me to a time when I was afraid about food security. I make a note about that. Then I think about what I have done with these gloves. I think of the joy of digging up potatoes with my children, celebrating each one like buried treasure.

I go to the kitchen for a potato and bring it back to my desk, thinking about all the ways we cook and eat them, and how baked ones remind me of my mother. Then I remember Sinead O'Connor's song "Famine" and how I used to listen to it on repeat at university when I became interested in social justice. I search for it on iTunes, and listen to her raging about the Irish potato famine. I keep listening as she burns with the fact that people were paid not to teach their children Irish, and how that battered their culture and history. As I listen, I feel the activist in me rising, wanting to stand up and fight for something. I make some more notes.

Then I return to the potato and turn it over in my hands, studying its surface, noticing the dents for the eyes, and realize that I find it quite creepy that potatoes have eyes, and I imagine what it's like to spend your entire life underground, just to be dug up and boiled, mashed, roasted, or fried. Trying not to judge the thought, I make notes about that too.

I sink into the armchair in the corner of the room and remember the dream of a slower life that led us to moving to the countryside to have room to grow potatoes. That leads me to thoughts about planting ourselves in a particular place. I make some notes about that and go back to thinking about the garden.

I have a flashback of my youngest daughter holding a bunch of fat radishes in her muddy little hands, and then I have a physical heart contraction as I realize that someone else is eating those radishes this year, because we sold the house. I am floored by a rush of grief for that home, and I realize how we can grieve for all kinds of things: people, animals, places, lost dreams, old lives, or houses we loved and still miss. I write a few notes about that.

An ordinary object can take your writing to extraordinary places.

I think about the abundance offered by Earth, and our connection to it, and what we are doing to it. And I make notes about that, too.

All that in twenty minutes, simply from picking up a gardening glove. I had no idea where it was going to take me, but I now have a handful of seeds I can use as sparks next time I write. Sometimes I have an idea-gathering session like this. At other times I'll get as far as the famine, go deep on that and never make it to the radishes.

Try it for yourself. Pick a thing. Hold it in your hands. Think about your relationship to it. See what happens.

Dissolve writer's block

I had no idea of Yūko Kubota's age. She was my *reiki* teacher, so it would have been rude to ask, but I wouldn't have been surprised to learn that she is twenty years older than she looked. I was conscious of the sweat dripping down my back after a packed subway ride and a dash from the station to her apartment. Kubota-*sensei*, meanwhile, was cool and serene as she guided me step by step through the first day of my *Reiki* Master training. It was Tōkyō in August, and it was intense.

"Don't use your mind to control what you are doing," she told me. "Release, surrender yourself, and go with the flow of the energy. Take care of your heart and follow its vibration."

The word *reiki* (霊気) means spirit–energy. *Reiki* is a Japanese energy-healing modality, which shines a light on any imbalances in the body, so it can start its own process of rebalancing and healing from within.

Kubota-*sensei* continued, "The self we normally identify with is a fabrication of our ego. Your true self is like a pure background consciousness that offers forth its wisdom. Sometimes these directions can take a while to come through, but there are ways to access this wisdom by bypassing the mind."

Reiki is one such way. Fearless writing is another.

We can become blocked or drained for many reasons, including stress and exhaustion. We can also carry past criticism, assumptions, and beliefs in our bodies. These blockages can manifest in many ways, including physical pain, tightness, mental fog, circular thinking, numbness, or a frustrating sense that something is there but we cannot grasp it. Any of these manifestations can further feed the block, as can trying to think our way out of it. But after writing millions of words and supporting thousands of writers to write, I have come to understand that writer's block is not a problem we can fix by thinking harder.

Writer's block is an energy block. Shift the energy, shift the block.

*

With regular use of the rituals and practices I am sharing in this book, I rarely suffer from writer's block these days, but I know it well from experience. For me, blocks tend to show up in my physical body in three main ways:

The knot: a problem to unravel

If I am trying to grapple with a complex idea or reconfigure a project, my tangled thinking often shows up as a knot, usually in my stomach, shoulders or back. My natural tendency is to push, to research more, to think harder, to stay longer at my desk. But these just tighten the knot. Instead, when I back off and drop into my body, fully ground myself, and stop forcing, the knot finds a way to unravel itself.

The inkblot: an emotional blockage

When my writing bumps up against a long-held belief or story, or an old wound, I can sense a dense cloud pushing up against the base of my lungs, restricting my breathing or causing a dull ache in my heart space. It feels as thick as an inkblot, and on difficult days it moves up into my head and lodges itself behind my eyes. My instinct is to turn away or push it somewhere I can't see it. But that doesn't make it go away. Instead, if I turn toward it with compassion and write around it, or hint at it with words, even if I don't write it directly, in time it tends to dissolve.

The fog: an absence of joy

When I am trying to write about something I am simply unin-terested in, it shows up in my mind and body as fog. It can be hard to pinpoint a specific location, but my limbs feel heavy and my mind is dull. I cannot muster the energy to deal with it, and I procrastinate. But if I acknowledge the feeling and give myself permission to write about something else, the fog lifts and I don't have to abandon writing altogether.

These might be familiar, or your blocks may show up differently. If you feel stuck on the page, look for clues in your body.

When we are blocked, the pressure builds and we need to release it in some way: physically (like running, singing or dancing), mentally (like journaling or talking about it), emotionally (like crying, screaming or laughing) or spiritually (like through energy work, chanting or spending time in nature). Writing itself can help. There are times when it works to reframe the block as an invitation to get vulnerable and take a risk. Other times it's better to write about something else. Your choice.

On the final day of my *reiki* training, after a simple ceremony with an audience of three large houseplants, I was suddenly hungry for a rice ball and some chilled green tea. I left my teacher's apartment and headed for her local supermarket, ライフ (pronounced *raifu*), noticing a new lightness in my body and mind. On arrival I was greeted by a huge sign bearing the supermarket logo—four hearts in the shape of a four-leaf clover—above a friendly English slogan: "Thank you for coming to LIFE."

WRITE NOW #07

On a piece of paper, write about something heavy that you carry. When you have finished, screw it up, put it into a heatproof bowl, and set light to it carefully. As it burns, feel for a sense of lightness as you watch it transform. Once it has

▶

finished burning and the ash has cooled, add a few drops of water and mix well. Dip the end of a matchstick or paintbrush into the ashy ink and draw a symbol or write a word in your notebook.

Write about the experience of burning your words, how you felt about it, and what it represents. Perhaps speak of physics, or the impermanence of everything, or the hope of creating something new from the ashes of something else.

Take care of your body

Yoga is nonnegotiable when I am on a long writing stretch, and my mat is always the first thing I pack when heading off on retreat. Looking after our bodies helps deliver us to the page vital and ready. During a long writing session, it's important to take regular movement breaks, too. I often take a question for a walk, and return with an unexpected answer. One of my favorite ways to break up a long session at my desk is with a walking meditation, taking one slow deep breath for every step and paying attention to the feeling of my feet on the earth as I walk. I use an ergonomic chair, or, if I am working away from home, I take a portable back support, and I often stand up to write. Over the years I have come to understand that freeing up the body helps free the words within.

WRITE NOW #08

Today, pay close attention to the way you move through a particular space. Any space will do—it could be a room, a town square, a park. As you move through it, notice the following:

- What is underfoot and above you?

- What is changing as you move, as a result of your movement? (The flow of a crowd? The view? Your center of gravity?)

- What is the air carrying? (Rain? Dust? A fragrance? Good news?)

- What do you notice about your body as it moves?

- Slow your walking to the pace of one full breath to one step. What do you notice?

Make some notes, then keep writing for at least ten more minutes.

Move your body.
Free your mind.
Write.

Chapter 3

PRACTICING

鰯の頭も信心から
(iwashi no atama mo shinjin kara)

*Even the head of a sardine can
become holy with devotion.*

JAPANESE PROVERB

In a busy life, it's easier to make room for things when they lead to a clearly defined goal. We do this in order to get that. Perhaps that's why we often put pressure on ourselves to achieve something when we write, to justify the time. Write a bestseller by the end of the year. Get one thousand words written by the end of the day. Metrics and measurable progress rule our modern lives. But what if, in focusing *only* on them, we are missing the point?

Imagine if we practiced writing just to become more awake.

In many Eastern traditions, the point of practice is not actually to achieve something specific, or even to become more skilled at something. That is often the result, but it is not the point. The point is to become more awake to the experience. To notice what is happening. To listen to the world unfold.

*

"More awake" is not a specific measurable goal. To aim for something so vague is the antithesis of modern goal-setting culture, but just imagine if we did it anyway. Imagine if we wrote not to hit a word count, or tick a box on a habit tracker, but simply to practice, and in doing so to wake up. To open ourselves to the world and see what happens. What else might we notice? What else might we write? What kind of writer might we become? Let's find out.

This chapter offers a whole host of ways to find new things to write about, or new ways to write about existing things. I call this counterintuitive approach "writing with a sense of purposelessness," and it has been a revelation in my own work.

You never know which day you are going to have a breakthrough. You never know which sentence is going to be luminous. Often you don't even know where a particularly beautiful combination of words even came from. They just show up on your page, or in your day as you are doing something else. That's the unforceable element of mystery, and it's what happens when you practice regularly.

This doesn't mean that we shouldn't set goals or use planners. It simply means that we recognize the difference between writing *toward* a goal (in the distance), and writing *because of* a goal (which is breathing down our neck every time we try to write a sentence). This keeps the goal out of our writing space. We show up but we don't force—and magic often happens.

Be interested

My husband recently commented on how often I use the word "interesting." I hadn't noticed, but now I think about it, he's right. I use it as a marker to acknowledge new information or something I want to explore further. I use it in conversation to show that I am listening and would love to hear more. The English word "interesting" derives from Latin *interesse*, meaning both "differ" and "be important."[1] I'm always on the lookout for newness, and "interesting" is a mental note to myself that there is something to see here.

The equivalent in Japanese is *omoshiroi* (面白い), which is written using the characters for face or front side (面) and the color white, like a blank piece of paper (白い). The etymological dictionary *Gogen Yurai*[2] actually describes the breakdown of the characters as "in front of your eyes" and something being "bright and clear," pointing to the beauty right in front of you. I love this description. To stay interested in our work, we just have to keep paying attention to what is clear and bright in front of our faces.

We can do this by paying attention to what is unfolding, and we can do it by putting different things in front of us and watching what happens.

Take a blank screen or white sheet of paper, for example. Many a writing session begins with a blank page, and many a writer has rued the intimidation they feel when facing it, so what if we put something else in front of us?

Paper is not just paper in Japan. It is art and craft, tool and resource. It wraps chopsticks, gifts, food, spaces, and light. It is a sliding door, a repository for ink-brushed poetry, a folded sign of peace. Paper can be so many things, yet we tend to revert to writing on a flat white sheet, or a lookalike page on a screen. Changing the shape, color, and texture of the material we write on, and how the pen moves across it, can bring a freshness to writing that lifts us out of a slump.

Become the expert of the moment in front of you.

Try writing on the side of a paper cup, turning it as you write so your words follow its shape. Scribble in large letters on a used cardboard box. Unroll a scroll and write long sentences from one end to the other. Jot down ideas on a paper bag. Use a fountain pen, or a stick of charcoal. Change the size and shape of the letters or the intensity with which you write.

Pay attention to what happens to your words depending on your environment, mood or time of day. I find that if I write on a quiet morning in my study, my letters tend to be tiny and neat, but words spilled immediately after a dance session are huge and swirly. Notes from the road are scruffy and full of wonder. Those scrawled at a time when I felt trapped are hard to decipher. If the way we feel and what we are writing affects how our handwriting appears on the page, it's curious to experiment with changing our handwriting and see if that has an impact on how we feel and what we write.

The Gate of Desirelessness, *Muganmon*, is sometimes referred to by the alternative name *Musakumon* (無作門), which literally translates as the Gate of Randomness. This version of the name highlights the importance of not presuming control, and I love the playful twist.

It's very easy to get stuck in a rut. We tend to do that as human beings. There's something comfortable about a routine, and doing the same thing over and over can be a fantastic exercise in noticing if we pay attention to what is different each time—the weather, the people, the journey, our feelings. But when things are repeated so often that they become automated, we often stop noticing anything at all.

When this happens, it can be fun to break the pattern of what is expected. Think about how you do the things you do, and instead do the opposite, or try something different. Walk to work instead of driving. Eat dessert for breakfast and have dinner in the bath. Put on a hat. Talk to a stranger. On your coffee break go and sit in the park without looking at your phone. Drop a coin on a map and go there. Instead of writing at your desk today, climb a tree and write while sitting on a branch.

You can switch up your focus too. If you tend to write about everyday details, go big. The incomprehensible vastness of the universe. The way the moon, which looks so small to the human eye, has the power to move the ocean. The sheer volume of the things that we don't know.

If you tend to write in the abstract about huge topics such as love and loss, try the opposite. Get specific. Notice ordinary life as it is. Write about the queue at the post office, a tin of baked beans, the plumber who won't stop talking. Or try a new format. If you tend to write poetry, try a factual how-to. If you usually write recipes, write a love story instead.

Ditch the routine and see what difference it makes.

WRITE NOW #09

Think of something you regularly do a certain way and do it differently today. Write about what you notice or discover.

Seek out newness

Don't stagnate. Surprise yourself. Give yourself opportunities for newness. It could be as simple as taking your notebook everywhere and noting down anything curious, profound, or beautifully ordinary: what you learned from a hushed conversation, what you discovered at the park, what happened when you turned left instead of right. Walk through your day with your eyes wide open, anything is fair game, and soon you'll have a notebook filled with observations. Or seek out a new podcast or a new book and let it inspire you.

Abandon all notions of what kind of writer you think you are, and just write.

Sometimes I put my children to work for the sake of my art. We'll take it in turns to tell a story out loud, or we'll pull a book off the shelf, open it at a random page, read the first sentence we see, and start a new story there. It's a fun way to get used to the intimidating prospect of not knowing what is coming next.

The more you write, and the more you put out into the world, the more it can feel like you should write a certain way, or you should write about certain things. Indeed, there is value in getting known for something. But as a creative person, there are so many possibilities for you, and your words. Don't limit yourself.

Try showing up at your desk with an intention of finding joy in your work today. Remember, you get to do this.

WRITE NOW #10

Fill a bag with twelve objects from around your house. Don't overthink your choices. Pull out two objects and let your brain search for connections between them. Write for three minutes.

Add a third object, and write again. Notice how clashing random objects sparks new ideas.

Put those objects to the side, pull out two new ones, and repeat.

Make up words

Writing evolves all the time. I love peering back through history to discover the etymological roots of words. It's quite freeing to notice the evolution of language and realize that as writers we get to play a role in that. We can take it one step further and give ourselves permission to create our own words, or clash words that don't normally fit together and use them so well that the reader understands what we mean.

When I was writing *Freedom Seeker*, I was exploring ideas about community, and I noticed that I didn't identify either as an extrovert or an introvert. I thought about when I am at my most energized and creative, and I realized that it is when I am among a small group of people who, like me, come alive where the outer world meets the inner world—who are both practical and spiritual, challenging and yielding, gentle and strong.

I wondered whether there was a name for people like us. I discovered that someone in the middle of the extrovert–introvert spectrum is called an "ambivert," but to me it sounded like a cleaning product and I didn't want to be one, so I invented a new word to capture it. I'm a "kindrovert" (from "kindred" + the "overt" of introvert and extrovert).

We kindroverts light up among kindred spirits, buoyed by connecting authentically and nourished by sharing our thoughts with a quiet confidence when the vibe is right. We ask good questions and really listen to the answers. We are interested in other people's ways of life, belief systems, and stories. We soak up the moments and remember the details.

We often lack confidence, initially, but we can shine with the support of others. A few kind words in our direction can do wonders, and we can step into enormous power in the presence of other kindroverts. We'd rather make no new friends than make new superficial friends. We trust deeply and are eminently loyal.

You are the writer. You get to choose.

Not long after the book came out, a magazine did a whole feature on the idea of kindroverts, and I have received many lovely notes from readers identifying with the word.

If you can't find the word you need, make it up. When you start doing that, you start having all kinds of fun with language.

WRITE NOW #11

Choose any two words at random and clash them together to see if they could work as a new word or phrase. Give it a definition. Try it in a sentence. Have another go with some more words. Write a short story or poem that uses one of your word inventions.

Write memory

If we are honest about it, we never really have an excuse for not knowing what to write about. We are walking catalogues of memories and can reach in and pull one out at any time. If you ever get stuck in your practice, choose a memory, reach toward it, and see what it wants to show you.

Weather can be a good way in. The other day I woke in the night to hear rain on the thatched roof of our cottage, and I was nineteen again, lying on my futon at my homestay house in Kyōto.

winter rains drumming
laundry on the balcony
drenched in homesickness

So much of what we write is from memory, recent or distant. Memory is so important, and yet it's risky. Our memories change over time. We often cut out the painful bits and emphasize the good, or we do the reverse to add drama. We paste several memories on top of each other and treat them as one. We recollect a shared experience differently from the way someone else remembers it. It's not to say someone is right and someone is wrong. It's just what we do with memory.

It's interesting to ponder how much accuracy matters to you when writing memory. Sometimes entire stories hang together because of a single detail that you pull out, and there are times that inaccuracies could get you into trouble. But sometimes there is beauty in the haziness of it. Whether or not it matters that you were eating cherry pie when somebody knocked on the door depends on the context, and the story, and only you can decide.

Memory is fallible. You get to choose whether you fill in the missing pieces, make a feature of their absence, or write in a way that forgotten details don't matter.

Sometimes the writing becomes the remembering, and we realize just how much we have stored away. When I'm in the middle of an experience that I know I will want to write about later, I am always torn between staying fully present and hoping I will remember it, and noting just enough details that I can take myself back into the experience of the moment at a later time. I might take a photo or short video, capture sounds or voices with my phone, scribble a few notes in a journal, or send myself an email afterward to capture the most important things.

When it comes to writing something up later, photographs can be a huge help. I like to print photos and spread them out on my desk. I have a pile in front of me right now, from a research trip to Japan, and each one of them holds a thousand stories. I could write about what is in the photo and let that lead me to other things. I could write about what happened just before or after it was taken, or the cultural clues held in the visual details, or a conversation I had with the person in the picture, perhaps.

Sometimes we try to write about the past without a memory of our own, because we weren't there, or we weren't born yet. We have to scavenge for clues in all kinds of places, such as libraries or archives, or by interviewing other people, to construct imagined memories from what has been left behind.

In recent research I have been traveling to meet poets who lived centuries ago. I try to imagine what memories they might carry if they were alive today. I read descriptions of where they lived, study maps of where they walked, look at old paintings, learn about the state of the world in their time, find replicas of the kind of clothing they might have worn, and seek out diary entries from people who knew them. Of all of it, the clearest picture comes from the imprint they left with their own words. We can never know others completely, but we can build a picture from all these clues and then recreate it in our words on the page.

Remember, you are the one holding the pen. You get to decide which details matter.

WRITE NOW #12

Search "vintage photograph" in Google Images or find an old postcard of someone. Give them a name, and imagine their life. Write about them: age, job, family, home, lifestyle, fears, secret dreams. Then fast-forward a few decades and write what became of them.

Be interested.
Have fun.
Write.

Chapter 4

OPENING

一華開五葉
結果自然成
(*Ikka goyō o hiraku.*
Kekka jinen to naru.)

A flower opens up five petals.
Results blossom naturally.

JAPANESE PROVERB

My first paid writing commission came from *Wanderlust* magazine in 1996. I was living in Japan and had decided to travel home by train with two friends. We were going to fly to Beijing, then join the Trans-Mongolian railway as far as Moscow, connect into the European rail network, and then take the new Eurostar back to England. It was a grand plan, except that we didn't have any money. We got busy earning however we could. We cashed in the return leg of our flights and taught English in the evenings, but our student visas limited how many hours we could work. I remember sitting on a floor cushion at my low desk trying to make the numbers stack up, when a copy of *Lonely Planet Japan* caught my eye. Of course: I could be a travel writer. Surely it just meant writing about places far from home, and I was already far from home, so I could write about that and sell my words. The next day I used the school's computer to send an email to the editor of *Wanderlust*, pitching an idea to write about the Kurama Fire Festival. She said yes and offered a fee that would go a fair way toward the flight to China and the visas I would need. Writing suddenly became an enabler for adventures.

It's fair to say that for a while I saw that as the moment I became a writer. The external validation. The money in the bank. But actually that can't be true, because I had to have written for a long time to be in a position, at the right time, to land the commission. When I trace it back I find newspapers I made with my friend Kirsty when we were seven, play scripts I typed on my dad's typewriter at nine, a poem about a tramp published in the school magazine at twelve. Flicking through the five-year diary I kept in my early teens I realize the truth: I have always been a writer. And I suspect it's true for you too.

The moment you opened your eyes to the world, you became a writer. From the first story you dreamed up and put on paper. From the first time you noticed beauty or realized you see things a little differently from other people. From the first time you chose to write something down, instead of letting it pass you by, you have been a writer.

Don't let technical things like spelling and grammar get in the way. Of course it's worth working on them, or using technology to help you, but never let a lack of education in how to write well be an obstacle to writing.

Looking back now I can see that being a writer has nothing to do with other people's validation, having things published, or being paid to write. It is much deeper than that.

Being a writer is writing.

Being a writer is capturing things that spill from your head and heart, and putting them on paper.

Being a writer is expressing the human condition and experience of existence in words.

It does not matter what the topic is. Everything, in some way, connects back to this strange and miraculous life, so take a moment and look at what you have written in response to the exercises in this book so far. Have you expressed the human condition or experience of existence in words? Yes, you have. So are you a writer? Yes, you are.

Let's embrace being writers, without attaching to a specific idea about the way writers should be. Any identity is a construct of the ego, just as self-doubt is. If claiming an identity as a writer helps you make time to write, then sure, wear your badge with pride. But let's not forget, if we are truly working in service of the writing, we don't need any label at all. We just need to write.

Trace your origins

Everything begins at the edge of the map to here. Before we go any further, let's take a minute to consider where we have come from.

> *I come from the water*
> *Boats in my blood*
> *Salt in my veins.*
> *I come from the page*
> *A house full of books*
> *A street full of stories.*
> *I come from roast chicken*
> *On Sundays*
> *And teapots of tea*
> *Served up with love*

By a teacher
And a dreamer.
I come from effort
Disguised as luck
And enterprise.
From a rollercoaster
Of having
And not having
Of knowing
And not knowing
But always hoping.

This is my origin story. What's yours?

When someone asks you where you are from, how do you respond? Do you mention a place? What country, what city, what town, what village, what land do you come from? What people do you come from? Not just the people who raised you but the people who raised them, and the communities that surrounded them all. What choices and sacrifices do you come from? What serendipity and coincidence do you come from? What bravery and stories do you come from?

What is your origin story? And who is the "you" in all of this?

Show me your original face before you were born. Zen *kōan*

Exploring our roots, and getting a sense of the vast web of people and decisions and happenings that led to this point, can help us honor where we have come from and all that we have been through, while reminding us that what comes next is yet to be determined.

WRITE NOW #13

On a blank double page in your notebook, draw a visual map of your life up until this moment, focusing on the most important events, places, people, and experiences, including anything related to writing. If it helps, divide the space into sections for each decade of your life and try to map things chronologically.

On your life map:

- Connect related things with colored lines or by circling them in the same color.

- Add any observations about these recurring themes.

- Highlight turning points or key decisions you have made along the way.

- Trace the evolution of your writing practice onto the map, including when anyone discouraged or encouraged you.

Now tell me your origin story. Go as far back as you like and write in any style you like. Start with "I come from . . ."

Confirmation everywhere

Following a path without knowing or trying to determine the destination can be scary. We never know what is coming up around the next corner. It can be a real comfort to get some confirmation along the way. Ever since I started writing books, my path has been littered with signs and symbols that seem to support my choices.

I don't understand it, or know how it works. I just know that it happens to me over and over again when I open my eyes and look.

Let me give you an example. When I was writing the proposal for this book I had a wave of self-doubt. It comes with every book, but this one was very specific: *Who are you to write a book about writing? Millions of people write. What's so special about you?* This rapidly became: *You haven't written enough. You don't know enough.* You know how it goes. And then it got nasty: *You want to write a book about being a fearless writer, and yet look at you, doubting yourself. What a joke.*

At that exact moment a deck of affirmation cards jumped off the shelf above my desk and landed on my notebook. No word of a lie. My husband heard me scream. On the front of the deck it said: "I am enough exactly as I am." I took that as a sign to carry on, and here we are.

With *Freedom Seeker*, which has the metaphor of a bird running through it, and a bird on the front cover, it was all about feathers. One morning, when I was feeling overwhelmed by the amount of material I was trying to organize and had lost all sense of what the book was actually about, I opened my front door to hundreds of feathers on the front lawn. Walking to a café to meet a friend I was passed by a woman with a shaved head and a giant peacock feather tattooed across her scalp. My friend arrived wearing a feather-print dress. The barista had feather earrings on. I noticed when she was trying to shoo a trapped bird out of the café door. By the time the truck drove past the window with a giant feather painted across its side, I was laughing. You just couldn't make it up. Each occurrence was a much-needed reminder of what the book was about: the journey from trapped to free, of taking flight and soaring. I just had to stay focused on that and it would all come together.

You can read whatever you like into signs, but at the very least, know this: every sign you notice is proof that you are waking up.

> ## WRITE NOW #14
>
> Choose a symbolic shape, word or object that has some kind
> of meaning to you, such as a heart shape, the moon or the
> word "home." Look for it everywhere over the next twenty-four
> hours. Every time you see it in any form, note it down. Be
> open to seeing it in all sorts of guises. At the end of the
> twenty-four hours, write a poem or short piece inspired by your
> findings.

Opening to possibility

I often get asked how I find the answers to the questions I carry
when writing a book. Take *Wabi Sabi* for example. My research
mission was to discover the true meaning of the word and the
life lessons it held. I knew there were clues in the world of tea, so
when I was searching Airbnb for a place to stay in Tōkyō, I was
drawn to the listing of a small apartment that had been remod-
eled in the style and proportions of the seventeenth-century tea
room *Gen-an*, by contemporary architect Daisuke Sanada. When
I showed up to check in, Sanada-san and his wife Sayaka were
there doing the changeover.

We got talking about my project, and about *wabi sabi*, and
our conversation led to several introductions to specialists in the
worlds of architecture and craft, chats over coffee and thought-
provoking conversations around their kitchen table over the
course of the next few months. Sanada-san is descended from a
famous *samurai*, and I had seen his ancestor's suit of armor in a
Tōkyō museum. His historical knowledge, insight, and generosity

changed the trajectory of my research trips, and I will always be deeply indebted to him. Every book of mine unfolds this way, as a trail of questions, clues to answers, conversations, introductions, and discoveries.

When we open our hearts and minds to possibility, infinite inspiration awaits.

When we put questions out into the world and take some action without holding tight to what the result needs to be, things open up for us. People get delivered onto our path, hinting at the next step. We can bring this openness to our research—where we go, who we talk to, what questions we ask and how we listen for the answers—and also to the writing practice itself, actively seeking out inspiration but also being open to finding it in unexpected places.

This is the territory of "What if...?" spoken with a hopeful heart.

WRITE NOW #15

What burning question do you have about the world? Write it down. Make a list of the kinds of people who might offer clues to the answer (such as "an architect who designs tea houses" or "someone who has experienced a volcanic eruption"). What if you could actually meet someone like that? Imagine you have, and then write in the past tense about what happened and what you learned, as if telling a friend. Then think of one small step you could take today to make that opportunity even a slight possibility, and take it.

Travel companions

When we step out of the hermitage and back into our lives, it can be hard to explain what we have been doing. Ponderings about the mysteries of writing don't always fit in with the conversation at the school gates. Family members don't always get it. Not every good friend makes a good travel companion on the writing path. Not everyone understands a burning desire to write. Not everyone feels comfortable with the topics we want to write about. People might be cynical, negative or even critical about what we are doing. Our commitment to writing might feel threatening to them, or it might touch an old wound of unfulfilled creative dreams.

> People can love you without being interested in your writing.

Sometimes, showing an interest in someone else's dreams can help them to show an interest in ours, but sometimes we just have to accept that we need to look elsewhere for support. Being conscious about this means that we don't offer the wrong people our vulnerability when we are trying to write.

An essential part of becoming a fearless writer is building a network of people you can trust for soul nourishment, support, and encouragement, without criticism or any sense of competition. Find people who share an idea of success that is not about validation and fame but about experience, beauty, truth, and contributing to the world. Often those who really get it are those who are doing it too. They know what it means to keep showing up without knowing what is going to arrive. They know the importance of leaving the day at the door to enter the circle and write. They don't judge or criticize your writing to feed their own ego. They encourage you and celebrate and commiserate with you, as you do with them.

Like-minded, supportive people can be found in writing groups (where you show your writing) or support groups for writers (where the focus is on information exchange and moral support). New friends can be found on writing courses and retreats or in online communities. Podcasts about writing and interviews with other writers can remind us that we are not alone.

For every friend who falls away, a new one will arrive through the doors opened by writing, and those people are a blessing.

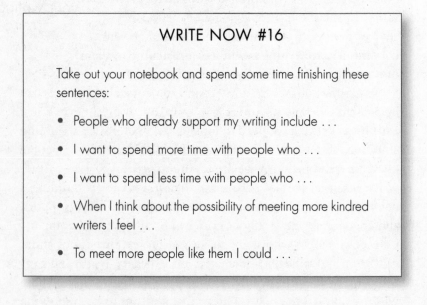

WRITE NOW #16

Take out your notebook and spend some time finishing these sentences:

- People who already support my writing include . . .

- I want to spend more time with people who . . .

- I want to spend less time with people who . . .

- When I think about the possibility of meeting more kindred writers I feel . . .

- To meet more people like them I could . . .

Living between the crisis and the still point

I am writing this on a Live Writing Hour with a group of writers from around the world. We meet twice a week for an hour. I light a candle, read a poem, say a few words, and we write together in silence. Sometimes I bring something to work on, but today I showed up with no plan. I just wrote this:

As writers we cannot exist only in the vicinity of crisis or still point. We have to know both the suffering in the outer world and calm in the inner world to process and cope with difficult things, and keep writing.

In a crisis we can use our words in many ways, depending on our expertise, our experience, and our proximity to the events. We can speak up for what we believe in, raise awareness of the crisis, show compassion to those suffering, offer a place for those in crisis to escape to in their imaginations, or offer tools to help. We can write through our own crises, or help others write through theirs. We can use words to reduce the separation caused by the splintering of communities, lives, and hearts. We can also open our eyes to the strength of the human spirit in times of difficulty and use our words to shine a light on that.

In order to stay open-hearted and connected to both the suffering and beauty in the world we need to live between the crisis and the still point.

To draw ourselves back toward the still point where we have clarity and objectivity, we can practice breathwork and bodywork, engage in deep listening, read poetry, take time out, and of course keep writing. This can help us to find stability again and reconnect to a sense of inner calm.

From the refuge of the still point we can use our words to offer solace, remind people of the beauty, good, and love in the world, and show them that they are not alone in their suffering. We can use our words to remind others and ourselves how we are all connected. But we cannot stay in the still point forever, or we become oblivious to life.

We go back and forth, eyes open, breathing deeply, bearing witness to the suffering and gathering the beauty, using our words where we can and where we must. This is part of our work as fearless writers. As we come into awareness of this, we know we are almost ready to pass through the Gate of Desirelessness and prepare for our initiation in Part Two.

WRITE NOW #17

How could you use your words to change the world, or impact the life of even one person?

Open up.
Calm down.
Write.

Ceremony at the First Gate

Here we are on the final approach to the Gate of Desirelessness. Let's take a moment to acknowledge all we have seen and experienced on the path so far.

We have learned how to quieten the mind and the noise of the world so that we can begin, and carry on.

We have learned to let go of the need to control what our writing becomes.

We have embraced whole-body writing and learned to take care of our energy.

We have practiced writing simply to become more awake.

We have learned what it means to be a writer, without attaching to any fixed notion of what that should look like.

And we have been reminded to live between the crisis and the still point, staying connected to both the suffering and the beauty in this world.

We are standing taller now, moving with a new lightness from all we have shed. As we cross the threshold of the Gate of Desirelessness I invite you to speak these words aloud:

> *I write. I express the human condition and*
> *experience of existence in words.*
> *I am a writer.*

At this crucial threshold, I offer you this:

> *When you speak these words fearlessly,*
> *May a distant bell sound for you,*
> *May the birds sing for you,*
> *May the mountains turn toward you,*
> *May thunder clap in a far-off land.*
> *May the act of saying the words release the need*
>   *to say them,*
> *And just as you claim your writer identity,*
> *May you release the label,*
> *And simply be what you are,*
> *And express that in words.*

May you see how ready you are to write whatever wants to be written and learn how to share it with the world.

Part Two
Initiation

The Second Gate: *Musōmon*

無相門

The Gate of Formlessness

To approach *Musōmon*, the Gate of Formlessness, we need to:

- Discover the essence of writing.
- Recognize what water can teach us about the creative process.
- Discern what writing is meant for sharing and who to share it with.

Only then can we pass through the second gate, and write and share our writing fearlessly.

Journey Note 2

Toward the Gate of Formlessness

"Did you know that Adelie penguins have affairs?" Fujiwara-san asked.

"What? No!" I answered distractedly from an armchair, which I was trying to keep from sliding across the ship's library by gripping the arms with my hands (pointless), and the wooden floor with my feet (more successful).

"Oh yes. Wealth in the Adelie world is measured in the number of stones they have gathered to build a good nest. The girls often fall in love with the poor-boy penguins, the ones with big hearts but few rocks. So they leave their mates to go in search of a puffed-up single penguin with an impressive store of house-building supplies, get it on, and then steal his stones for the nest they are building with their true love."

Kōichi Fujiwara is one of Japan's leading wildlife photographers. He was on board the polar ship to give a lecture about penguins, and lead us by a Zodiac boat to an island where we could see thousands of them in their natural habitat.

We became friends mainly thanks to my questionable

competence. I was one of a handful of volunteer interpreters on board *Peaceboat*, a Japanese NGO ship taking several hundred young Japanese people on a ninety-six-day voyage around the world. Not long out of university, I had little confidence in my abilities and believed everyone was better at the job than me. In fairness, they probably were.

While at sea we had to simultaneously interpret lectures given by visiting experts. In port we would accompany the Japanese passengers on local tours, sharing whatever the guide wanted to talk about: apartheid in South Africa, climate change in the Pacific, myth and mystery on Easter Island.

In our team meeting somewhere off the coast of Brazil, our boss Eric revealed that two of us would be joining a group of passengers on a side trip to Antarctica. They would leave the main ship in Argentina and join an icebreaker that would cross the treacherous Drake Passage and visit the only permanently uninhabited continent on the planet. I couldn't think of anything I'd rather do.

"We're going to do *janken* to decide," Eric said, referring to the children's favorite Rock, Paper, Scissors, Japan-style.

"Saisho wa gū . . . Jan ken pon!"

We kept going until there were just two of us left in the game: my fellow interpreter Maiko, and me. We screamed, and hugged each other. And then realized that we had nothing suitable to wear for the trip.

A few days later I was in a coffee house in Ushuaia, a bag of new oilskins and thermals at my feet, staring at a list of the experts who would be giving lectures on board—lectures that would need interpreting. There was a glaciologist, a marine biologist, an ornithologist; I couldn't even introduce them without my electronic dictionary, never mind recreate their teachings in Japanese.

Which is how I ended up spending many hours in the ship's library learning new vocabulary ahead of each day's lecture, and it's how Mr. Fujiwara came to adopt me, a bit like the ship's cat. I couldn't help noticing that he had something of an air of penguin about him, and I love penguins, so we became instant friends.

I wanted to do his lectures justice, so I'd ask him to tell me everything he was going to say beforehand, hence our conversation about adulterous penguins that day. I tried to focus as I battled with my sliding armchair. Not so Fujiwara-san. He seemed oblivious to the ship's rolling.

"How come you are so calm when the boat is heaving like this?" I asked, curious as to how he never got seasick.

"Oh, that is a good secret," he said, leaning forward. "I don't try to battle the waves, I imagine I am the sea." And that, I would discover, is not only excellent advice for crossing the Drake Passage but for writing too.

Whenever I try to find the words to explain what it *feels* like to write, I come up empty. I am aware of the irony of not having the words to describe the process of spilling words, especially in a book about writing, but that's how it is. I write, but sometimes it feels like I am written. It's as if the edges of my self dissolve, and the words enter where my skin used to be.

Alan Watts hinted at this in his book *Tao: The Watercourse Way* when he said:

We know intuitively that there is a dimension of ourselves and of nature which eludes us because it is too close, too general, and too all-embracing to be singled out as a particular object ... Our only way of apprehending it is by watching the processes and patterns of nature, and by the meditative discipline of allowing our minds to become quiet, so as to have vivid awareness of "what is" without verbal comment.[1]

Writing is as natural as the trees and the wind—and as essential as breathing. We can know it, without being able to explain it. To use language is to limit it, but writing is limitless in its depth and potential. A little like the *Dao*. A little like water.

> *early morning swim*
> *surfacing through fractured light*
> *salty offering*

Water is sacred. It can cleanse and purify.

> When we honor our writing practice as sacred, it can cleanse the mind and purify our intentions, as we shift the emphasis from pursuit and performance to gentle growth and flourishing.

Water is dangerous. It can cause devastation, as Gretel Ehrlich noted so poignantly in *Facing the Wave*, her portrait of Japan in the wake of the *tsunami*:

> Water bullies its way into the hearts of things. Its knife cuts loose the coiled lines we use to tie ourselves to what we know.[2]

Water is essential. We need it for drinking, thinking, staying alive.

Writing is essential. We need it for learning, healing, staying alive.

I'm at my friend Kyōko's house in snow country, legs crossed beneath the heated *kotatsu* table, looking out at the rice fields behind her home. Everything is white. It is so different from the silver of the mirrored paddy that flooded just a few months ago. I hear gurgling as Kyōko pushes down on the lid of the plastic water pot, then hands me a cup of green tea. I hold it with both hands to warm them. Since the *tsunami* they heat only one room in the house. The cloud of steam dissipates, merging with the whiteness beyond. The snow, the steam, the memory of the rice paddy, it's all there framed in Kyōko's window, and suddenly I have a realization about writing which makes everything make sense.

Here's my theory. Writing exists in three different states, which mirror the properties of water: the gaseous state, the liquid state, and the solid state. When we understand this, and learn to work with each state of writing, we can write without fear the majority of the time.

Writing is a formless animate being with its own spirit, which works with you to release chaos and beauty onto the page. At least that's what it feels like to me. We cannot fully describe it, because it does not have a fixed form. All we can really do is be with it, and work with it as it shifts between these various states. We become paralyzed by fear when we treat all writing the same, but by acknowledging these different writing states we can confine our various fears to one state or another, not allowing them all to flood our writing space all the time.

Let me explain.

> *Gaseous-state writing*
> *is what happens when we observe*
> *the mind chatter*
> *and write it out of the head*
> *onto the page.*

Gaseous-state writing, also known as journaling, is largely a release of the past onto the page—memory, regret, burdens we have been carrying—often mixed in with the dusty chaff of modern life—shopping lists, to-do lists, worry lists, all the other lists. We write in this way to process feelings, make a decision, or to empty a busy mind onto the page. Gaseous-state writing is for our eyes only. We serve this state as operator and scribe. (See Chapter 5 for details.)

> *Liquid-state writing*
> *is what happens when we focus deeply*
> *and open up to retrieve words and ideas*
> *from the wild place*
> *beyond our everyday tangle of thoughts.*

Liquid-state writing is the fluid territory of metaphor, poetry, and intuition. It is where we behold the world and attempt to write about it. Liquid-state writing needs to be treated with care. We may recognize its wild beauty and be tempted to share it too soon. We serve this state as witness and channel. (See Chapter 6 for details.)

Solid-state writing
is what happens when we consciously use the mind
to structure, restructure, edit, and shape our words.

Solid-state writing starts with a piece of our own work, which we whittle, shape, sculpt, and polish. We write this way to inform, instruct, educate or tell a story in a way that someone else can take in. This kind of writing is interested in the intentional crafting of sentences, paragraphs, essays, entire manuscripts. Ultimately, solid-state writing is destined for others. It is where laptops are invaluable—necessary even. It is the only kind of writing that benefits from feedback from a select group of relevant people. We serve this state as artisan and editor. (See Chapter 7 for details.)

I have noticed a tendency among teachers to dismiss gaseous-state writing because "It's just journaling" and to worship solid-state writing, hence our learned perfectionism. The liquid state, where much of our best, most truthful writing happens, is rarely taught. When I am working on a book I tend to spend around 10 percent of my time on gaseous-state writing, 60 percent on liquid-state writing, and 30 percent on solid-state writing. In between book projects the balance shifts closer to 40 percent gaseous, 50 percent liquid, 10 percent solid, showing that I am spending more time journaling and less time editing, but still half my time on deep writing.

All three states matter, and together they help us to free the mind, open up the channel to write from a deep place, and then prepare that work for sharing with the world.

The following chapters will help you to connect with the spirit of writing in each of these states. The further our writing is from a fixed form—in the gaseous and liquid states—the less we have to doubt and fear because it is not meant to be shared, yet. The closer it is to a fixed form—in the solid state—the more we have to shift from creation to curation (and heart preparation) as we ready our work for the outside world.

As writers, form matters.

Tangible, physical forms matter. They locate us in a space, and locate our readers there too. We perceive things with our senses and translate them into words.

Intangible thought forms matter. Beliefs and opinions color and inform our work. Memories and stories become our work.

The shape of our words matters too. Their sound, texture, and rhythm, individually and together, bring an extra dimension to a piece.

The Japanese word for form, *katachi* (形), represents more than the shape of an object. It considers the relationship between inside and outside, aesthetic and purpose, the materialization of meaning. It can refer to an action as well as an object. The *katachi* of writing considers the relationship between what is said and unsaid. It ties beauty to utility, and materializes the image in our minds so that we can release it onto the page. Writing "takes shape" with time and attention.

> This is the essence of writing, I think. To honor, and attend to, both the formlessness of our creative potential and the form of our written words.

But form isn't everything. Creative potential is formless. Imagination is formless. Every writing project begins as a formless thing, and that early formlessness is an essential stage in the project's evolution.

And so we begin our journey toward the second gate, 無相門 (*Musōmon*) The Gate of Formlessness. In Japanese, the characters for *musō* mean "no" (無) and "appearance" (相). No form. Formless.

> *Pondering form*
> *and formlessness*
> *is a way to transcend*
> *our conditioning about*
> *what we should be,*
> *how and what we should write,*
> *and what is possible for us*
> *in writing*
> *and in life.*

As fearless writers we can take an overwhelming formless fear and reduce it to a manageable form by naming it. By naming it we can work with it. And sometimes, just sometimes, we can sense the great mystery beyond the material world, which renders the fear meaningless and powerless, at least for a while.

The next four chapters represent your initiation as a fearless writer. You will actively release any limitations you have put upon yourself and set your writing free. You will cultivate bravery and you will practice writing difficult things.

By the time you reach the Gate of Formlessness you will be ready to write fearlessly and share your writing fearlessly. Let's go.

Chapter 5

EXPANDING

Be broken to be whole.
Twist to be straight.
Be empty to be full.

LAOZI, *DÁODÉJĪNG*, VERSE 22[1]
(INTERPRETATION URSULA K. LE GUIN
WITH J. P. SEATON)

Over the next three chapters we will explore the three states of writing: gaseous, liquid, and solid. These are states, not stages. Which state you write in on any given day depends on how you are feeling and what you want to work on. You can experience more than one state in a single session. You might warm up with one, then move on to another, or naturally find your writing switching between them. There is no right or wrong.

Awareness of these three states of writing can transform the way we deal with fear.

Gaseous-state writing is not intended for sharing with anyone else, so there is no need to be afraid of what people will think. Liquid-state writing is supposed to be spilled onto the page without any editing, so there is no need to be afraid of quality. Solid-state writing begins with a piece of existing work, so there is no need to be afraid of a blank page.

Here's a quick reference guide to explain the difference between them:

The three states of writing

	Gaseous-state writing	Liquid-state writing	Solid-state writing
Behavior of the words	All over the place, formless, like steam	Flowing in a particular direction, like water	Holding their form, like ice
Purpose	To calm a busy mind	To enter wild mind	To hone our words consciously
How do we do this?	By noticing what's going on in the mind, and writing it down	By focusing deeply and opening up to retrieving and receiving words	By looking objectively at an existing piece of writing and shaping it
What it looks like	Journaling	Deep writing	Editing
How to enter it	Open your notebook. Write with the intention of spilling what's on your mind	Use a ritual and/or a writing spark. Write with the intention of capturing whatever wants to be written.	Start with a piece of existing writing. Write with the intention of editing and shaping it.
Suitable for sharing?	No. Gaseous-state writing is private	Not usually. Liquid-state writing is raw and wild. It might be shared with a trusted group of writers, but it needs marination time, and to be polished before it is ready to share with the world	Yes, solid-state writing is usually intended for sharing with others

How to practice	Keep a diary. Write early in the morning. Don't judge what you write	Use your writing ritual regularly. Integrate body- and breathwork into your writing practice. Don't judge what comes out	Take classes in writing well. Develop a trusted group for feedback and support. Learn to trust your own opinion
Where to find out more	See Chapter 5	See Chapter 6	See Chapter 7

Gaseous-state writing

To enter gaseous-state writing we simply watch our thoughts arrive and write them down without judgment. The way in could not be more simple: open your notebook, observe what you are thinking, write it down.

What I call "gaseous-state writing" you might call "journaling." It is an uncontrolled release of stuff onto the page, usually written by hand. It is full of feelings and the analysis of those feelings. It's a kind of cleansing. Gaseous-state writing helps us to understand what needs processing and healing, and to use our words to do that. We can also use it to figure out a problem or work our way through a dilemma.

Just like steam, our thoughts expand to fill the container of the mind, which can make it hard to concentrate and create. Gaseous-state writing offers the page as an alternative container for those thoughts, which helps us to free the mind. When we see a thought pattern arising or an old story bubbling up, we can write it out of our heads. In this state the words move rapidly, often jumping from one topic to another. The scribbles on paper might lack form and structure, as disorderly strings of words rush in all directions. That's fine. It's not supposed to be neat and tidy.

Gaseous-state writing has three simple rules:

Allow everything.
Write anything.
Share nothing.

If you only do one thing inspired by this chapter, make it that you keep your notebook in your bag and write something in it every day. There is immense value in this for calming the mind, making decisions, healing, and later reflection. Everything we write is, in some way, based on what we have witnessed, heard, felt or experienced, whether personally or at a distance. The more we pay attention to what is actually happening in our lives, the more material we have to help us imagine what could happen, which gives us stories and ideas for the page. In this way gaseous-state writing can also help to feed the imagination.

WRITE NOW #18

Open your notebook and complete these sentences with absolute honesty:

- I am tired of . . .

- I daydream about . . .

- I secretly imagine myself as . . .

- What's sacred to me is . . .

- What I really want to write about is . . .

Listen to your life

The only time I have ever flown somewhere for a single day, I was in Geneva for a meeting when an Icelandic volcano erupted, spewing a cloud of ash over Europe and grounding all planes for several days. I had only my handbag with me, containing my phone, wallet, passport, a notebook, and a pen, so I bought some spare underwear and a wraparound scarf, and a one-way train ticket to Paris.

I had a rare sense of lightness about me as I walked for miles around the French capital, picked up art supplies from Sennelier (one-time brush supplier to Monet) and imagined another life.

When I got home I framed a piece of art I had made that weekend. It was the silhouette of a girl cut out of a map of the city, with words of freedom scrawled around her edges. I hung it on my office wall, and whenever I found myself drawn to it, I'd reach for the wraparound scarf, put it on, and remember.

I started writing a blog and studying photography. I asked for a sewing machine for my birthday and I cleared a space in my house to paint. Whenever I ventured toward art, something would flicker in me. I knew I needed to do work that was more creative than my job at the time. That's how my company Do What You Love was born. Over several years we worked with some brilliant partners to build a diverse portfolio of online courses that have helped thousands of people figure out how to find work with meaning, flourish creatively, and live well. I taught some of the courses, but mostly I was behind the scenes making plans, producing classes and building communities.

I loved the work, and there is a special buzz that comes with witnessing people step into their full creative potential. But when I became a mother and failed to take my foot off the accelerator, I ended up exhausted and burned out.

I started writing again to process the chaos in my head. It soon became clear that my yearning to create was still there, but the urge to make art had been replaced with a desperate need to feel free. Perhaps I was clinging to my vanishing sense of self as children took over my world, my heart, my brain, my days. Now I realize that all my writing is a way back toward the girl skipping through Paris with a bag of paintbrushes, dreaming words of freedom.

I kept writing, processing, exploring, and it led to the idea of my first book, *Freedom Seeker*. All through this I kept a journal, and looking back I can see how certain patterns and themes kept coming up over and over. I wrote my way through some major decisions, and uncovered what really mattered to me.

When you have been away and return home in a Japanese context, it is usual to utter the greeting *tadaima*, loosely translated as "I'm home." It is written 只今, with characters that mean "only now." This ritual greeting apparently emerged as a shortening of *tatta ima kaerimashita*, which means "I just came home," but taken literally I think this is fascinating. To equate arriving home with "only now" indicates a return to presence. Returning to ourselves and the world through our presence. Returning to the home of our writing hermitage, that sacred space in the heart, and just listening.

When we pay attention and take notes, we map a route back home.

On reflection I can see that writing books coincided with the huge transition of becoming a mother, and the development of a desperate search for silence. I doubt that is a coincidence. We have to listen to ourselves—letting our fears, dreams, love, and longing spill onto the page. This is where writing becomes a tool for personal growth and navigating change.

Remember, the way in to gaseous-state writing is simple. Open your notebook. Observe your thoughts. Write them down.

WRITE NOW #19

In your notebook, draw a grid of twenty blank squares (four columns across and five rows down).

In the first column, write five words that capture the feelings you have felt so far today (one word in each square). These could be short-lived feelings that came and went, or a general lingering feeling.

In the second column write something tangible that corresponds with each feeling; for example, if you had written "under pressure" in the first column, you might write "ticking clock" next to it in the adjacent column.

Then in the third column, write the opposite of each feeling you listed in column 1, in the corresponding row.

In the fourth column, write something tangible related to each of the feelings in the third column.

When you have completed the grid, circle the five words that stand out most for you and use them as a jumping-off point to write a piece about where you are in your life right now.

Document your days

Keeping a diary can be immensely powerful, especially when you are trying to establish a writing habit. Whereas a journal documents your thoughts, a diary documents your days. Of course, one can merge into the other, but the initial intention is different.

The premise of a diary is simple: something happens, we write it down. It is an invitation to notice what happened, or what is happening, and to turn that into words on a page. We sharpen the quality of our seeing, and uncover what interests us.

There are many ways to approach a diary. You can summarize the day in a single sentence. You can focus on words that lingered, recalling a particular conversation, a sweet utterance from a child, or a poem that moved you. You can make a note of things that made you smile, or that you were grateful for today. You can write about anything strange or unusual that you noticed. You can think of a person you came across and write down what you noticed about them. When you flick back through it, you might start to notice patterns or connections between things. Pay attention to these.

If you are in the middle of something painful, you can acknowledge it by documenting how it showed up in your day, without necessarily writing the thing itself. Even if you can't write *about* it right now, you can still show up to your writing desk and make lists, however random, about stuff that happened. *Put my car keys in the fridge. Felt numb. Have eaten nothing but toast for a week.* These are easy-to-forget details that can help you stay awake in the middle of chaos and pain. A year from now those details might be helpful if you want to return and remember. Of course, we can always write from memory, but it rarely captures the immediacy. We forget the details, especially the physicality of it: how our skin was on fire, how the humming of the fridge made us crazy, how it seemed like the volume had been turned up on the world.

Documenting our days makes us pay better attention to the ordinary details, which are the doorway to everything else.

WRITE NOW #20

Take yourself somewhere special for a treat. It might be for a quiet coffee and a slice of cake, or perhaps lunch or dinner. Go alone. Dress up a bit if you like. Take only your notebook. Talk to the server. Notice your food. Listen for the sounds of the place. Listen in on other people's conversations. Be completely present there. Ask yourself, "What is interesting here?" Write whatever comes up.

· Choose one stranger at the café or restaurant and write about them. Who are they with? Who have they loved? What do they long for? What do you see of your own life in what you notice about them?

Take stock

We often use the phrase "story of my life" in a negative context in order to make a point about something that happens over and over, like being let down by someone ... again. But in doing so we are using language to trivialize something important.

The story of your life is a precious, fascinating thing. It is a catalog of the experiences, environments, people, and decisions that have brought you to where you are now. And the best bit? You are holding the pen. You can decide how your story is told.

Often gaseous-state writing digs up things from the past and sets them swirling. Today we are going to tackle that head-on by writing the story of your life the way you want to tell it. If it helps, refer back to the life map you drew for Write Now #13. This can be a truly empowering thing to do. It is an opportunity to rewrite any old stories that have been holding you back, in favor of the greater story you want to tell. Take this time to recognize what you have been through and survived, and how you have thrived, and to celebrate where you are right now.

WRITE NOW #21

Imagine you are interviewing yourself. Ask yourself each of the questions listed below and try speaking your answers out loud.

- Which places have had the most impact on your life and why?

- Who have been the main characters in your story?

- What has been the greatest tragedy of your story so far?

- What has been the greatest comedy?

- What change, decision or dilemma are you currently facing?

- What is most alive in you?

When you have talked through each answer, pick up your pen and just write for a while (at least ten minutes) to see what bubbles to the surface. Look back at what you have written and if something feels particularly juicy, dive right into it and write for another ten minutes.

Then answer these questions:

- If your life story was a book, which section of a bookshop could we find it in?

- What would the book be called?

- What would the back-cover blurb say?

- Who would endorse it, and what would their quote be?

Gaseous-state writing:
Observe your thoughts.
Don't judge.
Write them down.

Chapter 6

FLOWING

Best to be like water.

LAOZI, *DÁODÉJĪNG* VERSE 8[1]
(TRANSLATION STEPHEN ADDIS
AND STANLEY LOMBARDO)

Women have been free-diving for lobster, abalone, sea urchins, scallops, and oysters off the coast of Japan for some two thousand years. Some of these women, known as *ama* (海女, literally "sea women"), dive well into their nineties, spending a significant proportion of their waking life beneath the waves. Watching footage of the women taking a deep breath and reaching into the murky depths, I felt an unexpected recognition of their work in my own.

When I am writing in what I call a "liquid state," I too take a deep breath and dive below the surface into murky waters, not knowing what I will find. I have a sense of where to swim, and feel toward what might be down there. I dive down, arms outstretched, hoping to discover a treasure in the depths. If I'm lucky, I'll find an oyster. If I'm really lucky, that oyster will have a pearl in it. The more often I dive, the better I get at finding oysters, and the more oysters I harvest, the more likely I am to find a pearl.

I know this kind of deep writing feels good, and yet I cannot describe it exactly, because I lose all sense of myself when I am in it. It's as if as soon as I dive below the surface I become the sea.

When the divers return to the surface, they let out a sound known as an *isobue* (磯笛), a sea whistle, so distinctive it has been recognized by the Japanese Ministry of the Environment as one of one hundred symbolic sounds of Japan.[2] This whistle is the release at the end of the dive. As writers, when we return to the surface with our catch of ideas and words, our sea whistle is our true voice on the page. It is the foundation of our own soundscape.

Dive deep enough and you'll get to hear the sound of your true voice.

Back on the surface I look at the catch of words spilled onto my page and I wonder where they came from. I find a sentence that sings, which I don't remember writing. A formless idea that I have been grappling with for days now has a shape. Somehow, I have pierced the moment in front of me and reached beyond it, to bring back something I didn't realize that I knew. This is what liquid-state writing can do.

It's also why having a sacred writing space is essential. When we are called back to the surface mid-dive, by a child's voice, a phone notification, or a pull to check email, the trance is broken. Our catch falls through our fingers back down into the depths, dragging the sound of the sea whistle with it. But when we have had the time and space to dive undisturbed, we return bearing valuable pearls, and the memory of the deep lingers like the taste of sea salt on skin. In the words of one *ama*, "This is a job without beginning or end."[3]

Liquid-state writing

Ultimately, writing is a way to express our truth. In order to get to that truth, we have to loosen up and let go of what we think we should write in order to allow what we know, deep down, we need to say. But this is difficult if we are so hidden from ourselves that we don't actually know what that is. When we are heavily influenced by the noise of the modern world, bothered by what other people think, concerned about how we measure up, and attached to what might happen to our words afterward (even before we have written them) it can be hard to hear what we truly want to write. That's why we have to learn to listen to what wants to be written.

When we are little and caught not paying attention, we are sometimes told to "use our ears." But that is just one level of listening. We can concentrate our awareness on our heart space and imagine physically listening from there. For me this is a little like sending out a sonar signal from the heart and picking up on echoes where it touches something deep in the world. To listen even more deeply we can bring our awareness to the largest organ in the body—our skin—feeling out into the world in every direction, allowing the utterances of the world to enter us.

Many moons ago I spent a slice of summer learning papermaking at the Awagami Factory[4] in Tokushima, where the Fujimori family has been making *washi* paper (和紙) by hand for eight generations using centuries-old techniques. Among artists and interior designers worldwide, one of the most popular of Awagami's papers is *Asarakusui*—a fine, near-transparent membrane with organic holes, run through with long hemp fibers for strength. Hold it up to the sky and the light pours through.

At the other extreme is the museum-quality *Hakuho*—a heavyweight art paper. Almost impenetrable to light, it lends visual depth to artworks and can be used as a printmaking surface, or even sculpted. Both are *washi* paper, but their appearance, properties, and uses are vastly different.

This is how I imagine our writerly skin. To truly listen to the world, and write about it from a place of truth, we have to thin our skin until we are almost porous so that the light can penetrate deep within. Later, when we want to share our words with the world, we will have to thicken our skin once more so that we don't absorb everything that comes at us. But for now we need to thin it, so we can feel our way toward what we really want to say.

In deep meditation, when the awareness and sense of self merges with the experience, it is known as absorption. Thinning our skin to write can have a similar effect. We go deeper and deeper in our writing to the place where we can hear what wants to be written. This is liquid-state writing. As soon as you realize you are in it, you aren't in it any more, but if you look at the evidence on your page, you'll know from the wildness in your words that you did indeed venture there.

To thin our skin so we can enter liquid-state writing, we have to listen deeply. This begins with a practice that shifts us into the body—breathwork, meditation, yoga, ceremony or a simple ritual. Then we need something to focus on—a question, a physical object, a poem, a memory, a writing exercise—and we listen.

We abandon surface description in favor of feeling toward meaning, allowing words and ideas, memories and imagined scenes, to swell and crash onto the page in waves. With liquid-state writing we reach toward all that we know without knowing how we know it, uncovering the great truths swimming in our bones. Conscious writing gives way to spontaneous writing. When we forget that we are writing, we are in the liquid-writing state.

We listen to the world, and it listens through us. The words behave like water, running deep, carving their own channel, flowing around obstacles, and joining us to the sea of everything.

Sometimes the lines on the page feel utterly of us, and at other times as if they came from somewhere else.

The words left on the page are often unexpected and unexpectedly potent. The more you do it, the more familiar the written words become, and in time you realize that their rhythm is the sound of your real voice written down.

Liquid-state writing directs our awareness at the utterances of the heart to reveal truth, insight, and wisdom.

When you go deep into liquid-state writing, the judgment filter is dissolved, so you write what you really want to write without any attachment to the idea of who the "you" is, which renders unnecessary any worries about what "you" should or shouldn't say. It's as if we become formless, no longer a person thinking about the writing. Instead we *become* the writing in its liquid state and the words simply flow.

WRITE NOW #22

Go for a walk and find a pebble, stone, rock, leaf, flower, piece of wood, or other gift from nature that you can pick up. Hold it in your hand and study it closely. Look for texture, colors and patterns, cracks and crevices. Think about what it is made of, where it has been and how it got here. Write about that.

Now breathe deeply, signaling your readiness to listen. Soften your eyes and look into your object. Sense its aliveness. Ask it a question. Write what you hear.

Knowing the unknowable

A couple of years ago I wanted to go in search of deep silence and had planned to travel to Yakushima in southern Japan. It is home to a primeval temperate rainforest containing some of the oldest living trees in the world. Instead, the COVID pandemic savaged my plans, Japan closed its borders, and I was left at home yearning for the forest. Then I heard that there was an immersive exhibition on at the Wellcome Collection in London, featuring photographs of Yakushima by French visual artist Chrystel Lebas.[5] Her images of the forest were taken at twilight with long exposures in order to capture great detail. The enormous prints were unglazed, lit from behind and displayed throughout a dark room scented like wet soil after the rain. As I moved through the installation I felt the trees reaching out of their frames toward each other, and beyond the gentle piped soundscape of birds, deer, and a babbling stream, a tangible silence hovered quietly. It felt like a living prayer.

Not all silence sounds the same. The cushioned silence of my favorite library sounds different from a bamboo grove at dusk when the tourists have gone. A gap in a nourishing conversation sounds different from a gap in a wild storm. Whatever kind of silence we are listening in to, we have to slow down and reach in. Whole worlds wait inside the spaces between sounds, but life is loud, and we have to listen carefully to locate them. I believe that this is why sages, poets, and writers have tended to be reclusive.

It's almost impossible to be an active member of modern society and listen this way all the time, but when we enter liquid-state writing, we can listen for the words beyond words, and retrieve the beauty that lies there.

In between liquid-state writing sessions we can practice this in

conversation. Let someone speak, and listen with
your whole body. Don't say anything as they talk.
Don't anticipate their answers based on who you
think they are. Rather, take in what they choose
to share right now, both the said and the unsaid,
as an inhalation. When there is a pause in their
words, exhale slowly, giving room for them to carry

> It can be hard
> to hear the truth
> beneath all the
> noise in the
> world.

on if they like, and to let them sense you're listening. Only
if they are still paused after your quiet exhalation, offer something
in return. Try having a conversation where you listen 90 percent of
the time and talk for 10 percent. See how different your experience
of the other person is when they are really listened to, and notice
what you pick up beyond what they have said. Then, when the
conversation is over, see what you can find in the space left behind.

WRITE NOW #23

Before you begin, find a beautiful poem and try recording
yourself reading it aloud. Then close your eyes and listen to the
poem at least twice. Respond on the page however you like.

Staying fluid

Liquid-state writing flows from the depths. It connects us to
the truth of things. Poetry can emerge spontaneously this way,
as can entire profound sentences. Whatever the topic, liquid-
state writing can help you get to the root of an idea before self-
doubt kicks in.

*

Sometimes, liquid-state writing leads me to particular phrases or metaphors that help give shape to an intangible knowing. At other times it leads me to concepts to explore, like the Three Sacred Gates in this book, which can become the bones of a whole project. These concepts seem to materialize from nowhere, but when I look back through old journals I see that I have often been carrying a nebulous form of an idea for some time. Liquid-state writing helps us give shape to formless concepts without fixing them yet. We get just enough information to sense what something is becoming.

Keep reaching, without forcing. Keep writing. See what comes.

Eight hundred years ago, in his *Mountains and Rivers Sutra*, Zen Master Eihei Dōgen told of one Chinese priest who said, "The blue mountains are constantly walking."[6] Considered with the logical mind, this is impossible. Mountains are solid. They can't walk. Considered the same way, our concepts and ideas are solid. We get fixated on them and think that they have to be a certain way, unmoving, unchanging. But even mountains change in time. All things arise and disappear in time. Everything is fluid. Seeing things this way offers a freedom in knowing that our writing can be whatever it wants to be.

The greatest threat to liquid-state writing is the urge to rush. We have to take our time, and trust. We may recognize the wild beauty of our words and be tempted to share them too soon. In my experience, almost all words written in the liquid state benefit from marination time and often some shaping too.

Don't expect flow in your writing to mean flow in the reading. Flow in the reading is actually a product of solid-state writing. For now, you are only interested in spilling fluid pieces of a watery jigsaw. This is not even a first draft. If you have to think in terms of drafts, think of it as a pre-draft, but the most forgiving treatment is not to think of it as a draft at all.

WRITE NOW #24

Allow your mind to wander to a place that stands out in your memory, or somewhere you dream of visiting but haven't yet been. Close your eyes, breathe deeply and allow yourself to travel there in your imagination. Don't just pick China for example, pick that evening in the old part of Beijing where you found a tiny street stall with upturned beer crates instead of chairs and ate the best Peking duck of your life.

What can you smell? Hear? See? Taste? What are the textures of the place? What is the dominant color palette? The ambience? How do you fit into the scene? Make some notes.

Now move away from your actual memory or imagined experience, to notice something else happening nearby. Let this happening change the mood of the place and the moment. Write that for at least ten minutes.

Now read back over your work and find the part that feels most alive to you. Dive back into it, writing from that detail for twenty minutes, reaching beyond it for an untold story. See where it takes you.

Deconditioning ourselves

Liquid-state writing is an extraordinary experience, and when extraordinary things happen to me, I have a tendency to question them. Did I imagine that, or make it up? But over time, as coincidences, serendipitous occurrences, and actual miracles have piled up alongside thousands of hours of liquid-state writing, I have come to see that our assumed ordinariness is just a result of conditioning.

Every now and then, when we open our hearts to write, and dissolve the walls that keep us blind to the great mystery, we get a glimpse of it.

I believe our burning desire to write books and compose poetry is connected to that glimpse, not being able to unsee what we have seen when we have opened to the world. When we have entered liquid-state writing, and the mechanized world has dropped away, things are shown to us and poured through us onto the page. Things we may not even remember having written, but we recognize like an ancient truth when we read them back. This sounds like some kind of hallucination. It isn't. It's just writing. Isn't that wild?

The more often we practice letting go of our obsession with form, of things being how we think they should be, and of the need to control how things unfold, the easier it is to access this wild place and reach toward what is waiting to be written.

WRITE NOW #25

Spend a couple of minutes observing your hands. Move them. Turn them. Open and close them. Write something about them, if you like.

Then think of an everyday ordinary activity that requires opening or closing, pouring, turning, carrying, pushing, or pulling. Write a scene in which someone does that activity, holding both the ordinariness and the miracle of it at once.

Reach into the deep place

There is a beautiful line in Stephen Mitchell's poetic translation of the *Dáodéjīng* (published under the title *Tao Te Ching*), which says "If you want to know me, look inside your heart."[7] This tells us that we are more like each other than we realize, but I also love to think of it as a recognition of what words can do. If we share what is inside our own hearts, it resonates in the hearts of others. Some might describe liquid-state writing as writing from the heart.

As a concept this can sound intimidating, because we tend to build walls around our hearts so that we don't get hurt. To share what we have hidden there is a radical act of vulnerability. If we do get a glimpse of what lies deep within, it can feel exposing to even acknowledge it, never mind share it. But every time we write this way we get closer to what is real and true, and when we have had a glimpse of that, it is hard to be content writing anything else.

What is real and true for you will be real and true for others too.

This is what it means to listen beyond the surface of things. Just as the breath is a bridge between body and mind, the liquid-state writing brought about by deep listening can be a bridge between ideas and words, guiding us to give form to the formless wisdom which swims deep inside. Perhaps, in time, we will share what we find, so others can know it too.

This deep listening, and deep writing, is an important part of the process, but it is not the whole process. There is a discernment that has to happen before we share our words. We have to assess whether our writing is ready and gauge whether the world is ready for it. It might be that the messy, beautiful truth you uncover with liquid-state writing is best shared as it is, or it might be better woven into a story, or edited for clarity—or kept to yourself.

This ability to differentiate between what is and what is not ready to share is a key skill for a writer who wants to leave an imprint on the world, without wounding themselves or anyone else in the process. We will get to this in Chapter 7, Shaping, and Chapter 8, Sharing. For now, keep diving back into the deep place, and see what else you find.

WRITE NOW #26

You are standing in front of a doorway. Visualize the door in great detail and notice whether it is leading out or leading in.

Depending on the type of doorway you have imagined, bend down and peer through the keyhole, or through some other narrow opening. What lies beyond it?

Make notes about:

- The atmosphere and feeling beyond the door.

- Any people or objects you can see.

- Any ideas that bubble up about the place, people or objects.

- Anything that is curious about the scene. What is she holding? Why is he crying? Why are they here?

Now tell a story of this place. Write for at least twenty minutes without stopping.

Liquid-state writing:
Tune in.
Go deep.
Write it down.

Chapter 7

SHAPING

In the pursuit of knowledge,
every day something is added.
In the practice of the Dao,
every day something is dropped.

LAOZI, *DÁODÉJĪNG*, VERSE 48[1]
(TRANSLATION STEPHEN
MITCHELL)

Years ago I wrote a masters dissertation on interpreting between Japanese and English for elite athletes in competitive sporting environments. In the course of my research I came across an obscure corner of linguistic theory that explores the nature of language through the metaphorical use of physics. Originating from research by Kenneth L. Pike, this corner of tagmemics discourse theory looks at how language behaves like particles, waves, and fields.[2]

Inspired by this we can consider how whatever we are writing about—an object, event, person, idea or memory, for example—can be considered as a particle (an isolated thing), a wave (a thing merging with and existing in relation to other things), or a field (a thing connected to everything else within a functional system). This can help us see an apple as an apple, as an ingredient in the apple pie we remember from childhood, or as one point in the great cycle of nature from seed to seed.

We can also use it when shaping our work. For example, we can review at the level of the particle (considering each individual word, sentence, paragraph, or section and its meaning, sound, and suitability). We can review at the level of the wave (seeing how it works in relation to the other words or sections around it). And we can view at the level of the field (considering how it works in the context of the book, article or piece we are trying to write). This allows us to zoom out to the overall idea and zoom in to the details.

Shaping language is both science and craft.

Besides this, one of the most important things I learned from my studies about interpreting and translation was that there are two elements to an effective transfer between languages. One is the accuracy of meaning, and the other is the impact of the language. The first is specific and technical, requiring extensive knowledge of vocabulary and grammar. The other is nuanced and emotional, and I think it's why so many accomplished translators make extraordinary poets.

I have noticed something curious about our sharing behavior. We writers often say that we are scared to share our work, and yet we often share it too early, inviting criticism for a piece that isn't yet ready. By "ready" I mean shaped in a way that translates both the meaning and experience we want it to offer. The way to avoid much of the fear and the criticism is by giving time and attention to solid-state writing before we share it with the world.

Solid-state writing

We have a tendency to trust other people's opinions of our writing over our own, which leads to us seeking feedback before we have properly reviewed the work ourselves. I encourage you to get out of this habit and build trust in your own solid-state writing skills. You are the only person who can see the image you are trying to render on the page. Learn to feed back on your own work *before* requesting feedback from anyone else, and you will find that you can share with more confidence when the time comes.

What I call "solid-state writing" you might call "revising" or "editing." It's revisiting and restructuring, shaping and sculpting. We start with a piece of our own writing—a paragraph, a page, a whole chapter—and we make it shine. Solid-state writing smooths our words to polished ice, and our work becomes a captivating prism that can refract the truth like light.

This is the territory of most writing courses and books. How to write better sentences. How to work on character and plot. How to structure your work. How to make it do this or that. We can hone our sculpting skills through practice, guidance, and reading of other work. Ultimately, this kind of writing is destined for others: to inspire, connect, educate, or narrate.

You know your work best. Start believing that your opinion of it matters.

There is much talk among writers about how hard it is to accept our first drafts, allow them to be awful, and carry on. Allowing them to be awful is good advice, but I'm not sure that bashing out a full draft early on then staring at it in despair is a particularly healthy way to write in the first place. Personally, I uncover what I want to write as I write, and it arrives in bursts. I write in fragments so small that I don't feel compelled to judge them in a way that I might judge a whole messy draft, and I use solid-state writing to hone each one. I later merge these pieces into longer sections, and merge those to create chapters, and a book.

In this sense I rarely have a blank page, because I capture

fragments floating in the breeze, pin them to the paper, and begin from there. When I come to weave all the pieces together into a full draft, those carefully shaped fragments feel like a gift from an earlier version of myself.

If you write fiction and feel compelled to spill the whole story in one go and edit later, try this: spill it, then put it away in a drawer and start afresh. Work on fragments for a while: a scene here, a conversation there. Polish the tiny pieces, and then feed them back into the longer piece. See how they lift it.

Of course, there comes a point where all the pieces have to be woven together, with chapter titles. It's only at this late stage that I have something I might call a draft. Perhaps this is just semantics, but we know how important words can be.

Solid-state writing brings up valid questions about technical skill, accuracy, and the quality of our research. We do need to pay attention to these if we intend to share our work in the world responsibly, but they are easily dealt with by way of dedicating time to honing our craft, taking classes in the mechanics of writing, working with editors, researching carefully, and even paying niche experts to review what we have written.

There are many layers to this kind of writing, from choosing what to take out and what to leave in, to making final decisions about word selection, and reviewing whether you have accurately rendered the picture in your head onto the page. As we do this primarily with the mind, our judgmental thoughts are never too far away, so it can help to have a focused process for assessing our own work. In this chapter I am going to offer specific questions you can ask yourself to help shape your work without getting overwhelmed by your own self-doubt.

One of the worst things we can do when looking at a piece of our own writing is to ask, "Is this any good?" It is much more helpful, and less painful, to ask specific questions that lead us to useful, instructive answers without making us want to give up altogether.

WRITE NOW #27

Take an existing piece of your writing and play with any references to time within it. Here are a few suggestions:

- Change the tense. Notice how that changes the feeling.

- Take a sliver of the action and write the unfolding of a minute in real time.

- Move the action further back or forward in time, to see it from a different age perspective.

- Reorganize your piece to reveal the action unfolding backward.

- Bring an awareness of passing time into the content of the piece.

- Write about the same person being in the same place but at a different time.

- Imagine time stopping in the middle of your scene, poem, or passage, and everything freezing for a moment. What do you notice?

During the course of my research for *Wabi Sabi*, I realized that the essence of its related aesthetic could be distilled into four key elements: utility, simplicity, beauty, and story. It is only in the writing of several books since that I have noticed how this also seems to be the essence of my shaping process.

We are going to take a look at each of these elements in turn.

You might like to choose an existing piece of your own writing, and view it through each lens as we go.

Utility

One of the most important questions we can ask ourselves when reviewing a piece of writing is this: does it do the job it is supposed to? Of course, to answer that question we have to understand what job it is supposed to do.

Every effective piece of writing delivers on a promise of change. That promise of change can be anything. Perhaps, as a result of reading the piece, the reader will know something new, have a new perspective or feel differently about something. They might understand the inner transformation of the main character and relate to it themselves. They might have learned a new skill, got to know a new place, or have been moved by poetry. There is no right or wrong kind of change, but if nothing changes, there is no story.

For example, the promise of change for this book is threefold. By the end you will be able to:

1. Accept fearlessly that you are a writer, without attaching to a certain way of being as that writer.
2. Write fearlessly and share your writing fearlessly.
3. Fearlessly live the writing life.

This book has to deliver on that promise in order for it to do the job it is supposed to do. Within that, each chapter has a promise of change. For example, by the end of the chapter you are reading here I want you to recognize and be able to do solid-state writing.

Within the chapter each section has a smaller promise of change, to help you move from here to there, toward the promise for the chapter and for the whole book.

This holds true for any piece of writing: a magazine article, a podcast script, a screenplay, a novel, an online course curriculum, even a poem that makes the reader notice something, or think about something in a different way.

It can be counterproductive to formulate this promise of change too early, or to cling on to it too tightly, but when we come to finalize a piece, identifying it and delivering on it are essential.

To view your piece through the lens of utility, ask these questions:

- What is your promise of change and does your piece deliver on it?
- When you have finished reading, how would you summarize what you have just read? Does that fit your intention?
- Of all the things you have read on the topic you are writing about, what is special about your take on it?

Simplicity

A famous food writer once told me that she charges a certain amount to write two thousand words, but three times that to write two hundred. Less is worth more. Just think how much can be said in a three-line haiku.

We have to be prepared to let any of the words go, in favor of keeping the ones that matter most.

We can ask ourselves: *If I were to explain this paragraph in one sentence, what would I say? Is it better to say that or keep the whole paragraph?* And for each sentence we can ask ourselves: *Is every word here essential? What happens if I take this one away, or this one?* There is no right or wrong, these are just useful questions to ask in order to strip away anything unnecessary and get to what really matters.

To simplify your own piece, read it silently in your head, and answer these questions, adding any of your own that will help you check for simplicity:

- What is the main message, and is it clear?
- What happens if you cut the first 300 words?
- Does the piece flow from one part to the next? Would moving or removing any sentence or section make it flow better?
- Is there any unnecessary repetition?
- Can any of the sentences or paragraphs be simplified, or shortened?
- Is every word necessary?
- What themes or threads run through the piece, and are they clear?
- What is the bite-sized wisdom here? (There is always something.)
- Have you offered more explanation than your intelligent reader needs?
- Have you given so much detail that there is no room for your reader's imagination?
- Is the piece too simple? Is it missing anything important?
- Is the reader brought back to the main message by the end?

Then read your piece aloud, and answer these questions:

- Do you stumble anywhere?
- Do you run out of breath anywhere?
- Do you get lost, bored or bogged down anywhere?
- Does it make sense (if making sense matters to the piece)?
- How do you feel after reading it?

Leave it for a while and then come back to it. Read it again, looking for ways to tighten it, neaten it, expand or compress it. I challenge you to seek out at least one more change that will make it work even better.

When I feel like I am getting close to a final manuscript, I read every single sentence out loud. It is a good way to check whether it really flows. It makes clunky parts more obvious, and it shows what is working, and what is not.

WRITE NOW #28

Take a recent piece of writing and edit it down to half its length.

Read it aloud, then halve it again, without losing its central meaning. Compare the three versions and see which you prefer.

Now summarize the whole piece in six words or less.

Beauty

Japanese ideas about beauty reach far beyond seeing and deep into experiencing. Our personal tastes describe only what is on the surface, but there is an emotional quality of beauty that lives beneath. Certain objects, places, artworks, and pieces of writing can make us sense the vastness of our own imagination, the passage of time, the cycle of life, and the mystery of being part of something much greater than ourselves. To me, writing that touches on these things has a special kind of resonance, regardless of the genre, style or subject.

Beauty lives in the details but alludes to the infinite.

We can find beauty in the rhythm or tone of a piece, as well as the words themselves. We can find it in the spaces, as well as woven into the texture of the sentences. It can be rendered as elegance, gentleness, passion, honesty, raw emotion. We can find it in the visible or invisible meaning, revealed on the page.

Taste is individual, so it is inevitable that not everyone will like your work. But if you can reach beyond the surface and capture a sense of the emotional beauty that lives beneath everything, your work might resonate more deeply and widely than you could imagine. One of my favorite *haiku* by Yosa Buson[3] speaks of long and lazy spring days piling up, making the past seem far away. He gives form to the formless by "piling up" the days.[4] For me that's often what beautiful writing does. It gives form to the formless concepts and truths of the human experience.

The single best way to make your own work more beautiful is to discover what beauty looks like to you. Read poetry. Read fiction and nonfiction. Read as widely as you can, paying attention to the response of your heart as you read. When you find a writer whose work truly speaks to you, read everything they have written. See how it has evolved over time. Study how they write and what they write about to get a sense of what it is in their writing that moves you so much. See what you can learn. And then go back to your work and seek out the beauty hidden there.

First read your work with new eyes, experiencing it sensually rather than looking at it conceptually or critically. Sense the atmosphere, the light and shade, the textures, the sounds and shapes. Enter it and see what you find.

Then ask and answer these questions:

- How important is beauty here, and has it been given sufficient attention?
- Where is the gold in this piece? What is resonant, alive, and compelling, or quietly thought-provoking?
- Where is the breathing space?
- What small changes could I make to beautify it, in my personal understanding of what beauty means?

Back in the 8th century, Indian scholar Bhavabhuti wrote a wonderful poem about how critics scoffed at his work, but he didn't care because he wasn't writing for them. It ends, "*I write these / poems for a person / who will one day be born / with my sort of heart.*"[5]

If we write what we know to be beautiful, and hope that it is one day shared with people whose hearts appreciate the same kind of beauty, that is enough.

Story

There are many great books on story as it relates to entire novels and screenplays. They go into depth about how things happen, how someone is affected, faced with a challenge to overcome and changed internally as a result. For years I thought this related only to fiction until I came to write a nonfiction book and realized that not only was the whole book a story but also that there were elements of story inside the fragments on every page.

If something changes, a story is born. Everything changes, so there are stories everywhere.

These micro-stories infuse our words with a sense of humanity, regardless of what we are writing about. Any legendary story is actually a cloth woven with the threads of many micro-stories, each holding its own truth or a clue to a wider truth. Our own lives are stories woven with such threads.

As you look at your piece through the lens of story, ask these questions:

- What story is unfolding within this piece?
- What happened? What or who changed, and how?
- Would adding something personal enhance the piece?
- Would a metaphor help, or is a metaphor getting in the way?
- Does the piece have a beginning, a middle, and an end? (Sometimes the end is revealed in a flash-forward at the beginning, but, regardless of order, the piece needs to travel somewhere.)
- What makes it memorable?

When you have done this, look back over your piece and see how it has been transformed by being viewed through the four lenses of utility, simplicity, beauty, and story. By practicing solid-state writing, you have become your own editor, without making it personal.

I see the honing process of solid-state writing like a cycle of eye, pen and heart. Read what's on the page. Make notes about what to change. Check in with how it feels. Repeat. Experience of reading makes it easier to step in to the cycle at the eye.

Experience of writing and editing makes it easier to skilfully use the pen. Belief and stillness make it easier to connect with the heart. All of them matter.

Collectively these processes can help you shape your words into something clear, engaging, purposeful, and beautiful. Keep practicing this and you will see your confidence grow. Take a moment to acknowledge how you have brought into existence something that did not previously exist. You have honored your formless ideas and gently coaxed them into form on the page. It is nothing short of a miracle. But it does not end there. Now we will prepare to share those word forms in order that they might be read by another and transform once again into a formless image in the imagination of your reader, who might then render them back into form as they speak of your work to someone else or take action inspired by your words. And so it goes on.

WRITE NOW #29

Write about your first kiss in five paragraphs. Then switch the order, moving the end section to the beginning. Rework it so that it makes sense, and cut it down to three paragraphs. What difference did that make?

Solid-state writing:
Distill.
Simplify.
Polish.

Chapter 8

SHARING

In the end, stories are about one person saying to another: This is the way it feels to me. Can you understand what I'm saying? Does it also feel this way to you?

KAZUO ISHIGURO IN HIS 2017 NOBEL PRIZE ACCEPTANCE SPEECH[1]

I think we all worry about what we write, and what will happen when we share it. We worry about hurting people, about not doing the story or the culture justice. We worry about stereotypes as often as we worry about clichés. We worry about what people will think of the work, and of us for writing it. The truth is we never know how our work will be received until it is out in the world. The one comfort is that if we are sensitive enough to worry about it, we are probably sensitive enough to know deep down whether or not our work is ready for sharing.

If you are nervous about sharing your work, here are three things you can do to help yourself prepare.

Firstly, get clear on what you are willing to share. Our reasons for expressing ourselves on paper often differ from our reasons for letting other people read those words. Sometimes the words just need to be written down. At other times they long to be shared.

Secondly, remember that not all sharing is the same. Sometimes we share our words to communicate something private to just one person. Sometimes we share with a few select people for their feedback, to help us write better. Sometimes we share our words with our own community, to connect, educate or inspire. Sometimes we go further, reaching strangers through our books and through other people's audiences. The further afield you go, the less control you have over who sees your work. Once you have released your words beyond your immediate circle of influence, they can take on a life of their own, and while that is not something you can control, it is something you can prepare for. This is both the joy and the challenge of sharing your words in the modern world.

This leads me to the third thing, which is to set your intention for sharing beforehand. Consciously or not, we often share our work in a way which serves the ego (to get validation, to appear smart, and so on). We make it all about us, so no wonder it feels scary. But when we share in order to serve the writing, or serve our readers, we have a different experience, and we get a completely different response. Try it.

Take the risk

Back in the days when I worked for the Yamagata Prefectural Government, I had to translate a driving theory test from Japanese into English, even though I didn't have a driving license. I still don't. I know, I know. It's late. How has it taken this long to learn, you might ask. I'll tell you the truth: because it terrifies me. And yet that fear makes no sense to my rational mind. Billions of people can drive, so why can't I?

I meditated on this for a while recently, and do you know what I found at the bottom of the huge pile of mud? The fact that I do not want to die, or for anyone else to die because of me. There, I said it out loud.

I want to grow old with my husband, see my children flourish, write many more books. And for more than twenty-five years I have carried the story that by not passing my test I am reducing the chances of me or anyone else dying in a car crash that was my fault, and therefore, by my logic, increasing the chances that I will get to do all the things I want to do. Along the way I have conveniently ignored all the things that I haven't been able to do because I can't drive, and I've taken away my own agency.

You can spend a lifetime writing and never share a word with anyone. That is a legitimate choice. After all, we don't know what will happen once our words are out in the world, and that makes us nervous. We worry, confusing the value of the work with our own self-worth: *Will they like it? Will they like me? Is the work good enough? Am I good enough? Are my words safe? Am I safe?* The things we fear happening might indeed happen, and it's more comfortable to avoid that possibility by not taking the risk in the first place. But just remember this: if you avoid the risks of vulnerability, you miss out on the rewards of vulnerability.

Choosing never to share anything denies you the joy of connecting with others, seeing the impact of your words, allowing yourself to be seen, and showing others that you see them. It's a choice that denies others the medicine you have to offer. It's a choice that denies you the reward of knowing that medicine helped someone. I promise you that, on balance, it's worth the risk.

This chapter is all about preparing to share. First though, take a moment to think about all the good things that *could* happen if you choose to share your work more widely. I'm going to leave you to think about that for a while. My driving instructor is waiting.

WRITE NOW #30

Open up to what good might come from you sharing your words. Do a short meditation, some heart-opening yoga, or dance to your favorite song, to the full extent that your body allows, claiming space as you reach and move. Then open your notebook and write "Sharing my words matters because . . ." and write for ten minutes.

See and be seen

Just as writing is a sacred act, so is sharing our words. I know from guiding thousands of people through writing courses, and from surveying more than a thousand writers, that one of the greatest barriers to sharing is a fear of being seen, and yet one of the main reasons that we want to share *is* to be seen.

Soon after *Freedom Seeker* was published I went on a small speaking tour in the US. On one stage, lit up by fairy lights on a dark snowy night in Colorado, I told the story of my eagle encounter. When the talk was over, a woman in the front row put her hand up. She was sobbing, and it took a while for her to find her words. It turned out that she'd had an equally strange experience that she hadn't been able to speak about until now. By sharing my words, I had helped her find a way to share hers.

Every time I get nervous about sharing something, I open up the "Kindness" folder in my inbox and read messages from people who have read my books and been comforted, or inspired to do something. I hope that one day you'll write to me and tell me about something you had the courage to share, which went on to help or inspire someone else.

Many of us spend our lives at pains to cover up our insides, keeping things to ourselves for fear of criticism and rejection. But stripping away the layers of conditioning and sharing what we find is how we let our inner light shine, letting others locate us in this crazy world. **Shine your light brightly.**

Over the years I have learned that it helps to separate the notion of "sharing" into distinct activities:

SHOWING I think of this as showing our (unfinished) work *to people we know and trust* with the intention of getting feedback, either for positive reinforcement or practical advice.

Example: reading our work aloud to a writing group or having it reviewed by a mentor.

SERVING I think of this as sharing our (finished) work *with other people, including people we don't know,* with the intention of offering a benefit to them.

Example: a newsletter (where we share for free) or a book (where we get paid to share).

SELLING I think of this as pitching the idea of our work *to a specific person* with the intention of inspiring them to commission or publish it.

Example: a magazine feature or a book proposal.

We are going to take a look at each of these in turn so that we can learn to share fearlessly what we have written so carefully.

WRITE NOW #31

Write in the third person about your fears of sharing your work; for example, Beth is afraid of X because Y. This allows you to step away, see a particular fear from a distance, and find more compassion for yourself—and perhaps even discover a new way to deal with it. Share a version of this with someone. Choose carefully who you share it with, and set an intention for sharing. It might be that you just want to voice your fear or that you want to seek their advice if they have dealt with something similar.

Showing

The other day my eight-year-old was preparing for a comedy performance in our lounge and said, "Get all your laughs up into your neck so that they spill out as soon as I begin." Smart girl. She was telling us exactly what kind of feedback she was after. All she wanted was positive reinforcement. No advice or critique, just laughter.

It seems so obvious to ask for what we need at a particular point in the creative process, and yet we rarely do it. Instead, we tend to shove our words nervously in the direction of anyone who will read them and ask, "What do you think?" The person giving the feedback may or may not be qualified to respond in any useful way. They may or may not be kind. They might bring their own issues to our writing. Without guidance they almost certainly won't give us the sort of feedback that will actually help us ready ourselves, or the work, for sharing more widely, because they have no idea what we need them to say.

Get clear on what you need, and ask for it.

It is important to be clear what kind of feedback we are looking for, who might be well placed to offer that, and what questions we want them to answer, so we get specific, constructive information *relevant to where we are in the process.*

A few years back I went on a residential writing course. Our first exercise gave me the chance to try something completely different from my usual style. I went all out creating an otherworldly scene of Christmas. It was a bit out there, and it was far from finished, but it had something interesting about it. We took it in turns to read aloud. When I had finished, I looked at the teacher, whose face was screwed up in disgust. "Ugh!" she said. "That is just nauseating. Next!" That was the extent of her feedback. I didn't share another word for the next two days.

As I processed what had happened, I decided that my lesson from the residential was how *not* to teach writing. I decided to create a series of writing courses that were the antithesis of that experience: supportive sanctuaries where no critique is permitted.

At first people find this strange, because they are used to getting critique when they show their writing to others. The problem is, when you create something in a class and seek feedback straight away, you get bombarded with opinions on work that is not ready to be reviewed. Those opinions often conflict, and sometimes sting, and you might find yourself picking your confidence off the floor, as happened to me on that retreat. Instead, students in my classes are only allowed to comment about how someone's work has resonated with them. They might simply say "Thank you for sharing" or "I was right there with you." They are not permitted to say anything negative, suggest any changes or give advice. These ground rules are simple, and unconventional, but the difference is incredible.

Given a chance to share without fear of judgment, people who have never had the confidence to show anything start posting every day. In the space of a couple of weeks, the quality of writing increases exponentially. This is a great way to show early work. In time, when we have worked on a piece a little longer, we might venture toward more specific kinds of feedback.

In my online Live Writing Hours, we go even further with the restriction. We write together in silence for forty-five minutes, then anyone who wants to share reads out a single sentence that they have written. No background, no context, no apology. They read it, we listen. I say thank you, and we move on to the next person. It's fascinating to get a glimpse into what they have been working on, and it's liberating for us to share without fear of judgment or criticism. Try it with your own writing buddies, or come and join one of my sessions.

HOW TO GET USEFUL FEEDBACK THAT YOU CAN TRUST

If you have only just written something, don't seek feedback, only encouragement. Once you have shaped a piece as far as you can, identify someone who has the relevant skills, experience, background, or personality to give the feedback you need without bringing their own agenda to your page.

When asking for their thoughts, feel free to let them know how honest you want them to be (for example, "Be gentle" or "Be completely frank"). If you don't need them to check your grammar and spelling, tell them. Proofreading slows the reader down and it's harder for them to see the whole piece.

Give them specific questions to answer, like these:

- Which parts resonated most with you and why?
- What was your main takeaway after reading it?
- How would you describe it to a friend?
- Does it flow and does the order make sense?
- Which parts are working well?
- Is there anywhere you got lost, confused or bored?
- Is there any unnecessary repetition?
- Is it missing anything?
- Do you have any lingering questions after reading it?

When the feedback is returned to you, remember that it was given in response to specific questions you asked. Don't argue with the person who just gave up their time, at your request, to help you. Instead, see it as an opportunity to make your piece even more compelling, knowing that whether or not you take their feedback on board is up to you.

You can also offer to give feedback to writer buddies, asking them what they need and only offering that. In this way you weave trust between you, and start to build a supportive network that will help you all thrive in a new writing world of your own making.

Serving

What if you knew that simply by sharing your words, you could lift a spirit, mend a heart, save a life? What if you knew that someone's entire trajectory might change because of something you wrote? What if you knew that there is someone in the world who desperately needs to hear exactly what you have to say? All of these could well be true.

You can serve the world by administering your words like medicine.

As you begin to serve others with your words, make a point of collecting some of their responses along the way. Create your own scrapbook showing that not only does your writing matter to you but it also matters to other people. This is not about reviews of the quality of your work, but evidence of the impact of it. This will be a friend any time doubt rises again.

When we write from a deep place, we inevitably draw on our own experience. That experience might involve other people, who may or may not be happy to be written about. There are many ways to tell the truth as a writer. For me, it comes back to intention. Why are you sharing? If your intention is revenge on someone who hurt you, that is not sharing from a place of service. But if your intention is to help or inspire others, there will be a way that you can tell it which does serve. Don't just think about what might drop away from your life if you go ahead and share. Think of what goodness might sweep in.

There is a chance that what we write might shatter other people's long-held views of us. This can be a danger, an opportunity, or of no consequence, depending on how you look at it. It's fully possible that some people might not recognize the version of you who shared your words, and that can be difficult for them. People may be reminded of their own unfulfilled creative dreams, as yours are coming true, and that can be painful for them. But their response is not your responsibility. In the end it comes down to this: When the last page is turned, what will you wish you had written?

WRITE NOW #32

Pick one of the prompts below and respond to it however you like.

- Tell me about hope
- Tell me about your accent
- Tell me about chocolate cake
- Tell me about the woman in the red hat
- Tell me about loneliness
- Tell me about luck
- Tell me about your suitcase
- Tell me about the last fight you had

Then consider how your words might be medicine for someone else.

Selling

To make money from your words, you often have to sell an idea first, and write later. This is how most nonfiction book deals work, as well as many print and online magazine commissions. Now is a good time to thicken up our skin, and look up and out, to see how our work might live in the context of a marketplace. We then have to sell the idea to someone who can help us get it there.

This requires us to describe our idea in a clear, compelling way so that a busy publishing professional, like an agent or an editor, can see what we want to create, understand where it fits in the market, and, in the case of the publisher, make a decision about whether or not to take a financial risk on it. It is up to us to make that decision as easy as possible for them.

There is a paradox at work here, because we have to be able to articulate our formless idea in a neat and tidy form that someone else can understand, without forcing it into a fixed shape too soon. This requires flexibility on our part to shape it enough to communicate it, and then later (after the book deal or commission) to let go of that shape so that it can become what it wants to be.

To sell your work it's not enough to know why it matters to you. You need to make it matter to others.

Commissioning editors know this is how books and articles get written, which is why it requires a great leap of faith on their part to buy into an idea that they know will, in all likelihood, evolve with the writing of it. It's your job to help make that leap of faith, by communicating your idea in a way that helps them envisage the book, and trust that you will deliver it, and then tell the world about it.

You need to be able to answer these questions:

- What's the essence of your idea and why does it matter?
- Why you?

- Why now?
- Who's it for?

Fiction is different—you typically need to submit a full manuscript, and it's the writing, plot, and characters that matter the most; however, even with fiction, being able to articulate the essence of your idea in a compelling way is essential to get someone to read the manuscript you have so carefully written.

Whether or not you get the deal or commission depends on many things, including whether it's a good fit with the person or company you are pitching to, whether they think it makes commercial sense, whether they have anything similar in the pipeline, and whether it's good timing for them. Some of these things are beyond your control, but there are elements you can take responsibility for, including making your pitch as compelling as possible, researching who you are targeting and pitching according to their guidelines.

If you do all that and get a rejection, you can be glad for it, because it wasn't the right fit, or the right time. There is a difference between something not being a good fit and something not being good. Don't presume that one suggests the other. You can try to find someone who is a better fit, or tweak the way you present your idea, or try again another time with a different idea.

I have received rejections countless times, from magazine pitches to podcast pitches, writing residencies to grant applications. *Freedom Seeker* was rejected five years ago by the same editor who has since commissioned four books from me. Rejection is awful, but it is often a good thing in the end if it means that you avoid working with the wrong people at the wrong time on the wrong idea or you miss out on an alternative opportunity that comes about only because the first pitch didn't go to plan.

Whenever your work is rejected, I encourage you to do the following:

1. Remember that it is not personal.
2. Ask yourself if there is anything you could have done to improve your chances of it being accepted. If the answer is yes, make a note for next time, or tweak your pitch. If the answer is no, be grateful that you found out early on that it was not a good fit.
3. Take action. Send your pitch to someone else. Get stuck into another piece of writing. Move your body. Make a gratitude list or carry out a random act of kindness. It works wonders for lifting the spirits. *Ki ni shinaide.* Don't worry. Rejection is proof that you are a writer doing the work.

WRITE NOW #33

Think of your favorite museum and choose one artifact from its collection.

Respond to the artifact in a way that connects it to modern life. See beyond the physical object to what it represents. What does it tell us about history and human evolution? How is it connected to contemporary issues? What questions does it raise? What can it teach us?

When you have finished, think of an outlet that might be interested in your piece—the museum's website perhaps, or a magazine on a related topic. Craft a pitch to sell your idea, and then pitch it!

It's not showing, sharing, or selling
your words that makes you a writer.
It's writing them.
Keep writing.

Ceremony at the Second Gate

The Gate of Formlessness is in sight. Let's rest here a moment and reflect on the steps we have just climbed.

We have learned how to thin our skin to hear the world, and to thicken it to share what we have written.

We have come to understand that writing is like water, and exists in different states, and that knowing this can help us to write under any circumstances.

We have seen how writing can help us to free the mind and listen to the truth that lives beneath the noise.

We have discovered that we have the capacity to dissolve the walls that keep us blind to the great mystery—and get a glimpse of it.

We have learned how to finish our work, shaping and polishing our words before we share them.

Some of this has been immensely practical, some almost magical. We are far enough into this pilgrimage to know that not everything can be explained, nor does it need to be. We trust ourselves more now. We trust our writing to show itself—and our hearts to show us the way.

I know it hasn't all been easy. I know how much courage it

takes to write the truth and share it. But you have done it, and you're still here, still writing. As we cross the threshold of the Gate of Formlessness I invite you to speak these words out loud:

I trust the process.
I trust my writing.
I trust myself.
I write fearlessly and share my writing fearlessly.

At this pivotal stage in the journey I offer these words to you:

May you dive for pearls so often that the sea whistle enters the soundscape of your life.

May you honor and attend to both the formlessness of your creative potential and the form of your written words.

May you release any lingering fixed notions about what writing is and embrace all that it can be.

May you move beyond the anxious call of the ego, to write whatever wants to be written, and to share whatever wants to be shared.

May your words become water and flow wherever they must.

And now, my friend, your initiation is complete. The hardest work is behind you.

You are ready to integrate all you have learned, and start fearlessly living the writing life.

Part Three
Integration

The Third Gate: *Kūmon*

空門

The Gate of Emptiness

To approach *Kūmon*, the Gate of Emptiness, we need to:

- Open our hearts and minds to the idea that we are not separate from one another or from the world around us, but rather intimately and inextricably connected.
- Recognize the impermanent, imperfect, and incomplete nature of everything.
- Embrace writing as an intrinsic part of our lives.

Only then can we pass through the third gate and fearlessly live the writing life.

Journey Note 3

Toward the Gate of Emptiness

"Welcome to Yamadera," said the monk. "Is this your first visit?"
Actually, I lived nearby and regularly climbed the mountain temple's thousand steps to drink in the air and the views. It was a very special place. Yamadera was founded in 860 and visited by *haiku* poet Matsuo Bashō in the late 1600s on his famous journey to the deep north. He rested there awhile, and penned one of his most famous poems:

> *stillness —*
> *sinking into the rocks,*
> *song of the cicadas*

Matsuo Bashō, translation my own[1]

I found a quiet place to sit and took out my notebook to write a *haiku*. There on the same mountain, listening to the descendants of Bashō's cicadas, looking out over the same valley, drawn by the same impulse to write, I felt a strange sense of overlapping time.

Of course, where Bashō might have brushed his ink onto mulberry paper, I scratched my words into a notebook with a pen. The grass sandals of his day had given way to the hiking boots of mine. Somewhere in the distance was the concrete-and-glass government building where I worked, and beyond that Zaō, a volcanic mountain range, still bubbling with the same natural hot springs, but now boasting ski slopes where rough mountain passes used to be.

Writing of his visit, Bashō said:

> Monks at the foot of the mountain offered rooms, then we climbed the ridge to the temple, scrambling up through ancient gnarled pine and oak, smooth gray stones and moss. The temple doors, built on rocks, were bolted . . . The silence was profound. I sat, feeling my heart begin to open.[2]

I suddenly felt so small against the mountain that had held the temple for centuries, and the tunnel of silence reached back through time to the moment he wrote those lines. I felt the years between our lives shrink to a single breath, with gratitude for the great poet's presence and an unexpected, unfathomable grief for his absence.

Everything connected and nothing remaining the same.

In the course of researching this book, I carried out an in-depth survey of over 1,100 writers from more than forty countries, which revealed that many of our fears are universal. We fear being seen, judged, ostracized, or ridiculed, and we fear both failure and success. All these fears arise from a worldview that sees us as separate from one another.

The assumption behind each of these fears is that other people, even those we love, exist as judge, critic, and competition. This is totally natural in the materialistic society in which we live, which pitches us against each other with a "survival of the fittest" mentality. But it is devastating for our creativity and confidence.

If we can shift that worldview to one of connectedness, where nothing exists independently, and everything is delicately woven in with everything else, all those fears fade. We exist because of each other. We need each other to exist. We are waves in the same ocean. In Buddhism, this teaching—that all things are empty of their own inherent existence because they are all related to other things, causes, and conditions—is called 空 (kū), often translated as "emptiness."

The *Kōdansha Kanji Dictionary* gives 空 (kū) a definition of "the nonexistence of matter and self, the transcendental void."[3] According to the Japanese dictionary *Kōjien* it means that everything is connected and nothing lasts forever.[4]

Vietnamese monk Thich Nhat Hanh described this beautifully when he talked of how a piece of paper has a cloud floating in it, because "Without a cloud, there will be no rain; without rain, the trees cannot grow; and without trees, we cannot make paper. The cloud is essential for the paper to exist. If the cloud is not here, the sheet of paper cannot be here either."[5]

He went on to remind us that the logger who cut the tree and brought it to the paper mill is in the paper too, as are the logger's mother and father. We could extend this to say that every grain of rice the logger has ever eaten, which gave him the strength to do his work, is in the paper too. And we can extend beyond that and see that everything is only possible because of everything else.

This brings to mind an image of Naomi Miyazono, a young baker from the rural town of Ayabe, carefully placing a grain of rice into the palm of my hand and asking, "Does it feel alive?" I was in the area researching slow living for my next book and was having lunch in Naomi's tiny café, Koku. Naomi uses rice flour to make bread and cakes that are naturally gluten-free and says that when you hold freshly harvested rice or freshly picked vegetables in your hand you can feel the aliveness in them. She spoke of how energy in our food is connected to the life and energy in our bodies in a way that made me sense the dedication of the farmers and the inheritance of the land in the rice grain in my palm. I saw a web reaching outward from that one rice grain across the fabric of her entire community and beyond it into the world through me being there on that hot summer's day, listening, and now being here sharing it with you. Everything connected.

> *In the beginning was the Dao.*
> *All things issue from it;*
> *All things return to it.*

> Laozi *Dáodéjīng*, verse 52, translation by
> Stephen Mitchell[6]

When we live and write from the ego, separate from each other, our lives are a constant commentary on what we and others could, couldn't, should, or shouldn't do or have done. Emptiness is the absence of narrative.

According to Zen teacher Dainin Katagiri:

Before your individual thoughts, feelings, or perceptions arise and you reflect on yourself, wondering who or what you are, something is already there. Something is already alive. What is it? We call it big self, real self, or true self, but actually it is the vastness of existence. In Buddhist philosophy we say emptiness.[7]

Emptiness is an expression of the fertile void from which everything arises and to which everything eventually returns.

It is the experience of seeing through our fixed ideas about separate selves, and instead recognizing that everything is interconnected at the most fundamental level. In some traditions, this invisible "place" where everything is before it is, is called the *Dao*. In others it is known as the "fertile void."

"Fertile void" has also been used in psychotherapy to describe a phase of not-knowing, where there is uncertainty but also possibility, and I have heard it used by creatives in my own community to speak of the resting time between projects, when they are composting all that they have previously created or ideated but didn't use, readying themselves to bring forth a new painting, book or other creative project. It is the place from which all creations arise and to which the remnants of all creations return, to become seeds for new ideas.

Whatever our personal faith and beliefs, contemplating this can help us open up to the idea that we are not limited by the boundaries drawn by the ego. If we pay attention to what we are truly feeling and experiencing in the world, and notice how we are connected to everything else, we begin to live and write from the heart, open to life in all its great mystery and possibility.

All our doubts and fears are contingent upon our reality being based on a fixed sense of individual self. Contemplating the idea that something else could be true can be a powerful antidote.

We see this immediately when we return our attention to the

notion of our self in the material world, and the limits appear again: *Who are you to think that you could do that? You aren't smart enough. You don't know enough. You aren't good enough. You might as well quit already.*

But we are ever-evolving creatures, born out of an ocean of potential, and if we can carry these ideas with us, and keep reminding ourselves that perhaps our fears and doubts are constructs of our own ego, we can find relief, and perhaps even discover possibilities we had never previously imagined.

Beneath this idea of emptiness is the fundamental truth of impermanence, known in Japanese as 無常 (*mujyō*). Everything arises and returns to this vast void of creative potential. Everything is always arising, becoming or returning. Nothing stays the same. This can be very freeing as a writer, as we will discover on this last leg of our journey.

This final stretch is about integrating writing into the rest of your life. Over the next four chapters you will become an apprentice to the craft, explore the vastness of your own potential, deepen your writing, and consider where you might like to travel on the road beyond the gates.

By the time you reach the Gate of Emptiness you will be ready to live the writing life fearlessly.

Chapter 9

APPRENTICING

歩歩是道場
(*hoho kore dōjō*)

Every act is training.

ZEN SAYING

There is an old Zen story about a man who had apprenticed for a decade before becoming a teacher. One rainy day, he went to visit Zen Master Nan-in. On arrival, the old Master asked him, "Did you leave your wooden clogs and umbrella in the entranceway?" He had. "Did you put your umbrella to the left of your shoes, or to the right?" The man could not recall and realized that he hadn't yet reached full awareness, so he became Nan-in's pupil and studied for six more years to accomplish every-minute Zen.[1]

Apprenticing takes time. It is not just about practicing a skill but about developing the skill of practice. The word "apprentice" comes from the Latin *apprehendere* "take hold of, grasp" and the Old French *aprentis*, "someone learning." In Japanese the word 徒弟 (*totei*) is commonly used for "apprentice," which literally means "student, little brother." It has an interesting synonym, 門人 (*monjin*), which literally means "gate person." The writing apprentice is constantly crossing a threshold between the known and the unknown, as the boundary of the known expands and a new unknown comes into view, like seeing the mountain beyond the mountain. The verb 見習う (*minarau*) is often used to describe what an apprentice does—it literally means "look and learn." We look to other writers and mentors, and we learn. We read other writing, and we learn. We read our own work, and we learn. We look out at the world, and we learn. We look inside, and we learn. This is the writing life.

Being a writer is a lifelong apprenticeship to writing.

This road we are walking is neither straight nor easy. We do not just plod along for a few miles and reach the end. There may be warbling birds in a bush to the left, a beautiful tree worth inspection on the right, bandits up ahead. We might stop at a roadside tea house and receive a story from a stranger, get a stone in our sandal, bend down to remove it and notice one ant carrying another to safety. We continue on our way, changed a little. We cannot wait until we are perfect, because we will never get anywhere. If I had waited until I was the writer I want to become, I still wouldn't have published a book. I wouldn't have learned what I have learned from finishing each book and moving on. Each one has been possible because of the books that went before it.

The work of the apprentice is to do your best, and to know what is good enough and to let that be good enough. Each time we finish a piece of work and release it into the world, we come back to the writing desk anew, not as an expert now, but as a beginner at a new level of competence, ever the gate person, ready to learn.

We began this journey with a single step, and we continue it one step at a time, exploring one moment, one change, and one word at a time.

One moment at a time

In his commentary on the classic text *Instructions for the Zen Cook* by Eihei Dōgen, Kōshō Uchiyama wrote, "Living now does not mean a directionless living for the moment. In Buddhism, the present includes both past and future. To express it in simpler terms, I am speaking of a present which contains direction, wherein you prepare tomorrow's gruel tonight."[2]

When I write today, I prepare the gruel for tomorrow. I don't know what tomorrow will bring. I don't know if my idea will reveal itself as a book, whether someone will pay to read it, or if anyone will like it. I don't know exactly how the story I'm writing will end, or whether the question I am carrying will get answered. But I do know that writing now will be good preparation for whatever comes next.

When I find myself too caught up in thoughts about what might and might not happen, I like to write *haiku*. One of the most popular forms of poetry in the world, *haiku* differ from a lot of poetry by being focused on what is happening in the outer world, rather than what is going on in your inner world.

A *haiku* is a heartbeat-sized poem. In writing one we capture a moment. In reading one, we enter that moment. A *haiku* poet sees the stoniness of a stone, the treeness of a tree. To write a *haiku* we have to slow down and tune in to the world around us. Veteran translator Jane Reichhold has described a *haiku* as a "word nest" built to protect our inspiration until a reader can experience it as poetry,[3] cradling the memory of a moment in the way we might hold a baby bird. I love how this explains not just what a *haiku* is, but what it can do.

In theory, a *haiku* is very simple. It is a very brief, seasonal 17-syllable (5-7-5) or three-line poem, which accurately describes what is happening in front of the poet. Usually, two of the lines are connected to one main image, and the third line offers a contrasting or connected second image. Reichhold calls these a "phrase" and a "fragment" respectively. In terms of position, the fragment can appear in the first line or in the third.

Usually written from direct experience or memory, not imagination, a *haiku* can capture anything from the magnificence of a starry sky to the tiniest movement of a butterfly's wing. *Haiku* poet Matsuo Bashō famously said, "To learn about the pine, go to the pine. To learn about the bamboo, go to the bamboo." We know something by experiencing it, not just by thinking about it.

> Look at the world through haiku eyes and see it just as it is.

When we write a *haiku* we see something ordinary anew, and write it. We abandon ourself to participate in the world—sensing (seeing, hearing, touching, smelling, tasting) rather than feeling. A *haiku* does not speak of loneliness, it tells of a crow on a bare branch at dusk in autumn.

HOW TO WRITE A *HAIKU*

First read some *haiku*, pausing after each one to let it sink in.

Go outside with your notebook and a pen. Breathe deeply, quieten your mind, and tune in. See what is interesting. Rotate through your senses and make notes about what you can see, hear, smell, taste, and feel (touch). Put a couple of those images together and connect them. Don't personify things, or analyze or interpret. Just write what is.

Capture the moment in a tiny three-line poem. Write some more.

Tips:

- *Haiku* often include specific seasonal references. In Japanese these "season words" are known as *kigo* (季語) and often refer to plants, insects, the earth and sky, weather, or other natural phenomena. When writing in English, you can use Japanese *kigo* for inspiration,[4] or you could try a word representing something local to you and the season you are in, such as blackberries or a cactus.
- *Haiku* are not about the poet, they are about what the poet sees with all their senses. *Haiku* rarely bring attention to the writer. In English, the easiest way to do this is to avoid using the pronoun "I."
- Write in the present tense to bring the reader into the experience.
- Keep it simple. Drop most adjectives and adverbs. Write things as they are.

One of my favorite translations of one of my favorite *haiku* goes like this:

> *a bee*
> *staggers out*
> *of the peony*

Matsuo Bashō (translation Robert Hass)[5]

Different people receive *haiku* in different ways, but for me I am drawn to the personality of the bee, a bold, bright image against the delicate pastel beauty of the peony, a symbol of early summer. The detail of a bee staggering is a surprise. It makes me look more closely at the flowers in my own garden. Although Bashō wrote only what he saw, as a reader my mind carries on beyond the poem to conjure up an indulgent image of being drunk on the sweetness of life. This poem has a *nioi*—a fragrance—reminiscent of the flower itself.

To borrow a phrase from Japanese philosopher Kitarō Nishida, there exists in the poem a "continuity of discontinuity" with the juxtaposition of the blooming peony that will soon fade, and the act of a bee visiting a flower in full bloom, which happens over and over again in nature. Without saying so directly, it reminds us that change is the only constant. All in three simple lines.

WRITE NOW #34

Write three *haiku* using the guidelines above. If you like, include one of the following seasonal words (inspired by the Japanese year in the northern hemisphere) or include a seasonal reference of your own.

Spring mist, spring rain, skylark, frog, blossom

Summer wisteria, nap, cicada, heat, summer festival

Autumn moon, scarecrow, deer, persimmon, falling leaves, bonfire

Winter north wind, snow, badger, wolf, hibernation

One word at a time

In life, people become experts by narrowing their subject focus. As writers, we might have a particular area of expertise, or we may have to become a micro-expert on many things as our topics change from project to project. I have found that the least intimidating way to approach this is to narrow that focus to a single word. From there everything else can follow.

I have a tendency to write books that focus on a particular concept that can be hard to define: freedom, *wabi sabi*, Christmas, writing. As a list of themes they seem disconnected, but there is a thread running through them about doing what you love and making the most of this precious life.

One of the first things I do when I am working on a new project based around a particular word is to ask questions about what the term actually means. I explore it from every angle, considering my own experience of it, others' interpretations, its etymology, its context in different traditions, and so on. I look for a universally recognized definition, and when I can't find one I become even more interested.

With *wabi sabi*, I used to tell myself: *I'm just trying to move toward an idea of what it represents without expecting to reach a fixed definition.* That helped appease the voice asking who I was to think I could define a Japanese term that does not even appear in the Japanese dictionary. The way to do it was to see all the connected pieces of culture, history, conversational norms, and people's experiences that intertwine to bring meaning to a word, and then to reflect on what perspective that multilayered meaning might bring to our lives. Tracing a single word out to the vastness of all it can represent, and back to the simplicity of that single word, is excellent training for a writer.

When you choose a particular word and approach it in this way, you develop your sense of the subtle and the nuanced. You find new ways to explain things, and you start to see just how closely everything is connected. You don't have to be writing non-fiction to do this. In the context of fiction you could explore the central theme of your story. What is betrayal? What is longing? What is joy?

WRITE NOW #35

Pick a theme, ideally a word with more than one meaning, and write it down. Do some research about your word, using books, online sources, and your own experience, and by asking people that you know:

- What does it mean in your first language?

- What is the equivalent word in any other language familiar to you? Ask some native speakers for their understanding.

- What are the etymological roots of the word? How has it changed over time?

- Are there any common misconceptions about the word? Dive into any gray areas.

- What is challenging about the word or what it represents?

- How does the word change with circumstance or usage?

Now imagine that you have been commissioned to write 500 words about your one word for a new book about curious words from around the world. Find what is most interesting in your research and start there.

Being original

After a series of coincidences pointed me in the direction of the Westcountry School of Myth on Dartmoor, I found myself studying at the feet of Dr. Martin Shaw, one of the world's finest mythtellers. According to Dr. Shaw, "myth" means "no author." He says that these kinds of stories land deeply within us because they have passed like water over stones through many communities and lives. Myths ripple beneath our skin, splash over our bones, and merge our own despair and difficulty with all that has flowed before. Hearing a myth told well feels like a remembering.

I joined the school with no expectation. I just turned up with my sleeping bag, and my notebook, and I listened. I listened to wild poetry and song, to drums and smoke and the crackle of fire, to ancient myths told and retold. When I returned home I looked back over my notes, only to realize that I had written them all in pictures. It was the strangest thing.

I went back to the school on the moor several times that year, fascinated by the unconventional, radical nature of it all. My writing started to shape-shift, and reach into wilder places. Exposure to unauthored myths had challenged my ideas of what it means to be original.

The character for "book" in Japanese (本) also means "origin," "root" or "source." Books were traditionally seen as the root of knowledge. They also carry wisdom, stories, inspiration for living. To offer something original, I think we have to have an awareness of what has been written already, study and honor that, and then step away from it. We can look at our own origins and life experience, or we can tune in to the world of the formless—emotions, memory, intuition, dreams, imagination—and see what we find there.

*

There is a Japanese term for the three stages of learning that make this possible: 守破離 (*shu ha ri*). It is used in the tea ceremony and in some martial arts to describe the path of learning from beginning to mastery. First, we learn the fundamentals and traditional techniques (*shu*), then we start to bend the rules and innovate (*ha*), perhaps allowing ourselves to be influenced by a particular style, and then finally we go our own way, guided by the heart (*ri*). This is how we grow as writers and it is how we shape each of our offerings with integrity into something that feels original.

The more we practice, the more we can discard what we have learned from others and go deeper on our own ideas.

WRITE NOW #36

Take your notebook somewhere quiet among trees, or near water, ideally at dawn or dusk. Stand tall, feet rooted to the earth, arms up and out, palms facing forward, heart open. Take a few breaths here and settle in to the space. When you are ready, speak to the land, out loud, in any language of words or sounds. Then listen.

Write whatever you hear. Write some more. Read back what you have written and pinpoint the essence of it. Shape that into a powerful statement that feels original to you.

Then acknowledge the land that inspired what you have written.

Look and learn.
Notice what's happening.
Whatever happens, keep writing.

Chapter 10

AUTHORING

案ずるより産むが易し
(anzuru yori umu ga yasushi)

It's easier to give birth than to think about it.

JAPANESE PROVERB

For me, anyone who writes is a writer. But being an author is slightly different. It requires taking a book-sized risk. When I say "book" in this chapter, I am referring to any large writing project intended for widespread distribution, which includes nonfiction books, novels, screenplays, poetry collections, and so on, whether traditionally published or self-published. When I say "author" I mean anyone taking on such a project.

The main reason projects like these are so scary is that we authors have a tendency to attach our self-worth to the success of our work in the marketplace. There are so many things wrong with that it's hard to know where to begin, but let's start with the building blocks of a writing life.

In a small town called Onomichi, overlooking the Seto Inland Sea in Japan, there is a spa hotel with an extraordinary wedding venue in its grounds. Designed by Hiroshi Nakamura, the Ribbon Chapel[1] is formed from two giant interwoven spiral staircases rising up through the trees like a wooden homage to the double helix. But, unlike in DNA, in the case of the chapel the spirals join at the top. This building is what I think of when I think about the writing life.

We schedule our days as if life is linear, and we celebrate first books as the culmination of all our hard work, that culmination being an end point we cannot see beyond. But five books in I can tell you this: the writing life is more like a double helix than a straight line. One spiral represents our growth as a writer, and the other our growth as a human being. I imagine a thread running up through the center of the double helix, representing the theme of our life. It's the thing we keep being drawn back to whatever we write. For me this thread is about making the most of this precious life. Take some time to think about what your thread might be.

Give a book everything, but don't make it everything.

Every book we write takes us a little further up the writer spiral, and the living, healing, and growing we have to do to get it written takes us a little further up the human spiral. There is a sculptural relationship between how we live and how we write. We see the central thread from all directions each time we travel around it.

Getting that first book, poetry collection or screenplay out in the world is a fantastic achievement, but it is not the end, neither is it the only thing that matters. It is simply one loop of this beautiful, miraculous helix that intertwines writing and life in a constant dance.

In time we see how stories, ideas, and inspiration live in everything around us, and how our lives are intimately intertwined with everything we ever write. Perhaps the longer we live the writing life, the closer the spirals get, merging like the staircases at the top of the Ribbon Chapel so that life is writing and writing is life.

I want you to know this before you saddle your idea with all your hopes and dreams, and the weight of your self-worth and future happiness.

Don't focus on "getting published" as your single end goal. Instead, meditate on "becoming an author" as an unfolding path, without fixating on any particular notion of what that should be like. Every point we reach on the double helix is only a temporary location, because we are always traveling around it, spiraling upward through writing and life.

Shaping a book idea

I grew up surrounded by books in every room in the house. The idea of writing one seemed completely out of reach until I realized this: every book in the world begins life as a vague idea.

It's the same with a film script, or a radio play. That delicate wisp of a thing hovering at the edge of your consciousness? That could be the seed of a book-sized project. Our job is to sense these formless, fragile ideas and encourage them to reveal themselves to us. By gently shaping such an idea into a proposal or synopsis, you open a door to some of the most fulfilling work you will ever do: the work of writing a book.

EIGHT WAYS TO SHAPE YOUR IDEA

Try all these methods quickly, writing down whatever first comes to mind:

1. **The Chit-Chat Method** Imagine a friend has just said, "I heard you are writing a book. What's it about?" What do you reply?
2. **The Movie Method** Pretend to be a film executive pitching the screenplay inspired by your book. You say, "Think of it as X meets Y with a dash of Z."
3. **The Endorsement Method** For nonfiction, think of someone who really inspires you. For fiction, think of a novelist whose work you adore. Imagine they agree to give you a quote to go on the cover of your book—usually fewer than fifteen words. What do they say?
4. **The Magazine-Pitch Method** Imagine your deal is done, your book is written and the publicist working on your project is pitching to a national magazine. Which magazine would that be? How would they describe the work to an editor, and what angle would they pitch?
5. **The Question Method** What burning question do you want to answer with this book, and why does that question matter?
6. **The Book-Doctor Method** Imagine someone walks into a bookshop and says, "I need a book about . . . that will . . ." The bookseller replies, "I have just the book for you. It's called . . . and it's over in the . . . section." Fill in the blanks, recommending your book.
7. **The Haiku Method** Capture the essence of your book with a three-line poem.

8. **The Big-Idea Method** Now you have spent some time coming at your idea in many playful ways, explain it as a single big idea in one sentence.

(Extracted from my online course The Book Proposal Masterclass)[2]

It's important to know that your idea will shape-shift many times right up until the moment you hit "send" on your final manuscript. Even so, trying to describe it succinctly at various stages of the process can really help you to understand it, and to articulate it to others. In my experience, however much the detail changes, the essence of the idea usually remains all the way through.

WRITE NOW #37

Once you have tried the idea-shaping methods above, have some fun playing with ideas for the title of your book.

Getting it written

Every author has their own approach to tackling a major project, but in my case writing a book is nothing like I thought it would be. I imagined it would involve showing up at a desk for office hours, writing over and over until I got to the end. It's actually way more interesting and varied than that.

*

Writing often looks like going for a walk by the river, taking a yoga class, or being curled up in an armchair reading. It looks like a deep conversation, a train ride, or a day in a museum archive. Depending on what you are writing, where you are in the process, and how you like to ideate, incubate, research, and create your work, writing can look like almost anything.

A lot of the time writing doesn't look like writing at all.

For me the manuscript tends to come together in a fluid nonlinear process of asking questions and feeling my way toward answers, zooming out to the structure and zooming in to the detail. For my nonfiction books I gather up everything I have been thinking, map out those ideas onto sticky notes, and collate them into groups of similar themes. I imagine these as chapters to give me some kind of early container for the ideas.

I'm open to lots of possibilities in the beginning. I have a good idea about what I want to know, what I already know, and what I don't know. Then I figure out how to fill in the gaps. This gives me a vague research map that usually leads to unexpected people, places, conversations, and perspectives.

I read widely, not just on the topic of the book but also tangential topics. I conduct interviews, dig through my archives of memory, and spend a lot of time gathering stories and clues to the answers I am looking for. This can get messy. I have to take plenty of notes and label them carefully. Along the way I work on fragments of writing: a story here, a paragraph there.

It often takes a while for the book to feel like it is coming together. And usually, just as I am getting comfortable with it, everything falls apart. I notice a major issue with the structure, or a huge missing piece, and I have to rethink everything. This can be devastating, especially when you have a deadline looming, but I know from experience that it always leads to a better, more profound version of the book.

In time, the essential narrative of the book reveals itself and I let the nonessential fall away. This narrowing is a vital part of the process, or the book would never get finished.

In the final drafting stage I might have fifteen thousand words of fragments and twenty thousand words of research notes for each 3,500-word chapter. This distillation process is the most intense time for me, when I work for hours at a stretch, leaving my desk only to go for a walk, eat, sleep or spend time with my family. It's also the moment the book reveals itself in its fully formed shape, and I wonder how I pulled it off, then I remember that I didn't do it all by myself.

WRITE NOW #38

For nonfiction Gather up all your ideas for your book and write them onto individual sticky notes. Group similar ideas together and notice what themes connect them. Imagine those as chapters for your book. Write the contents page for the book you might soon author.
For fiction Describe your story in two hundred words.

Birthing a book

Every author has their own working methods, and every major writing project requires different things, but it's true to say that all my books have seen the same phases of development. Understanding this can help you prepare and spread the workload.

THE PHASES OF BIRTHING A BOOK OR OTHER MAJOR WRITING PROJECT

Phase 1: ideation

This is the sensing of the idea, which can happen in a flash of insight, or it might appear as a recurring theme over time. You will likely have many more ideas than finished books or screenplays in your lifetime.

Phase 2: incubation

This is the period of gestation of the idea, which can take weeks, months, or years. It's important to hold the idea gently at this stage, and allow it to take shape without forcing it too soon.

For nonfiction, you would usually write a proposal at the end of this incubation period, prior to moving into the creation phase. Some authors are represented by an agent who pitches their proposal to publishers on their behalf, because many publishers do not accept unsolicited submissions. Nonfiction book deals are usually landed on the strength of the proposal, and the manuscript often comes later once that deal is done.

Phase 3: creation

This is when you actually write. This phase might include parallel research and writing, drafting and redrafting, and submission of the finished manuscript to a publisher.

For fiction, you would normally submit your manuscript along with a synopsis at this stage, either to an agent for representation or directly to a publisher if they accept unsolicited manuscripts.

Phase 4: production + beautification

In the case of a book, this phase involves post-submission editing, design, and typesetting; writing the blurb for the back; approving the front cover; and other activities that contribute to polishing your book and bringing it to life. For other writing projects, such as screenplays, there is of course a whole phase of filming and post-production here, which you may or may not be involved with.

Phase 5: release preparation

This phase includes everything you need to do before release, including planning the launch and lining up interviews, reviews, events, features, and other opportunities to bring your work to the attention of your own audience and to get it in front of other people's audiences.

Phase 6: publication

This phase covers the time from the day of release through to the end of the "launch." Depending on your own plans and those of your publishing partner, this can be anything from a single day to several months. During this time you will be outward facing, writing and talking about your work in many different ways.

Phase 7: rest and reflection

This important, yet often forgotten, phase is the time to celebrate, reflect on the journey of the work, make any notes about things to do differently next time, and to take a break. We can power on

▶

through for a while when an important deadline approaches, but we cannot power on through forever. Rest, recovery, and reflection are important for longevity.

Phase 8: cultivation

Even if you start on the next idea as soon as the previous one is out in the world, it's important to keep talking about your earlier projects. A strong launch matters, but the ongoing cultivation of that project over the long term can be just as important.

There is no "right amount of time" for each phase. It depends on many things, including your working methods, your personality, a publisher's interest and timeline, and the wider context of your life and what is going on in the world.

Looking at it like this, it seems like a lot, but these phases might be spread over several years. Each one has its own characteristics, challenges, and joys. There are also day-to-day administrative tasks related to writing, including contracts, taxes, paying bills, and so on, that go on year round. It's important to be aware of all that is involved so that you can manage your time and energy carefully and avoid overwhelm.

When it's tough, remind yourself that this was your dream and you made it happen.

WRITE NOW #39

Imagine your ideal release day for your book, screenplay, or other major writing project. Write in detail what you do and how you feel.

Storing treasures

I wrote nearly half a million words to get to the fifty thousand in this book. Years ago this would have bothered me, but not these days. The truth is that sometimes I simply have to write through a thousand words to get to the hundred words I really want, and I have finally come to accept that that's the way it is for me. Just because words don't make it into the final book doesn't mean that they are wasted.

There is a lovely town in the Japan Alps called Takayama which is often referred to as "Little Kyōto." Many of its old buildings are well preserved, and prominent among them are the *kura*, old storehouses. These days many of them have been converted into cafés, art galleries, and Airbnbs, but originally they would have been packed with treasures belonging to wealthy merchants. *Kura* were seen as status symbols. The larger the *kura*, and the greater number owned, the greater the wealth of the owner.

These days I think of my notebooks and files of research as my *kura*. They contain snippets of writing, ponderings, quotes, poems, and personal stories. The more I have, the wealthier I am, because of all the potential living in those pages. If I am stuck for something to say on Instagram, or I have to write an original feature for a magazine, I open up the *kura* and look for a treasure. If I

Nothing is wasted, ever.

had written a novel, the *kura* might contain ideas for short stories, bonus content or alternative endings to share with my most loyal readers. The *kura* is stuffed full of gifts from my past self to my current self, and I am grateful for all of it.

Write down "Nothing is wasted" and pin it to your wall as a reminder next time you have to cut a beloved character or scene from your novel, or you are wondering whether writing about your cat is a waste of time.

WRITE NOW #40

Open your notebook at random to a page with writing on. Find a sentence or idea that you have not yet shared with anyone. Turn it into a newsletter, online post or a feature that you could pitch to a magazine.

Serve your people

In the world of writing there is often hot debate about how much to consider your reader when writing. Some say write for a market, others say write for a single person. Some say ignore the reader and write what you want to write. I think it depends where you are in the process. My thoughts on this are based on authoring books, but they can be applied to all kinds of writing projects, from playwriting to blogging.

In the beginning, when the idea is floaty and vague, I am not thinking about readers at all. I am just allowing the idea to show itself to me. By the time I decide to shape it into a proposal I am ready to start paying attention to the ways its main topic is showing up in the world around me: how it is arising in conversations, how it relates to the news or emerging trends. I do this because it helps me locate where the project will fit and who it might serve when it is done.

As with any kind of major writing project, books do not exist in a vacuum, they exist in the context of all the other books in the world, just as a movie exists in the context of all the other movies, and a blog exists in the context of all the other blogs. If you want to land a partner (like a traditional publisher) to help you bring your idea to life, you need to understand this to convince them where it fits and that there will be a demand for it. This is called the *market*.

You also need to understand which kind of people will actually read it, so you can figure out where to find them to tell them about it. Those people are the *audience*.

Even if you plan to self-publish, your creation still needs a market and an audience, and your proposal essentially becomes the business plan for your project. I do this work for the book proposal, then when the book deal is done, I put it to one side and forget about the reader again for a while, and go back to writing.

When I am in liquid-state writing, I am not thinking about anyone. I am just writing what wants to be written. When I am later editing and shaping that, I am thinking about whether it is going to help someone make the change I am promising to them, so I have the reader in mind, while staying true to what the book wants to be. At this point, if I know what change I am promising, I already know something about my reader, because they must be someone who wants and needs that change. Then, later, when the book is done and I am thinking about how to share it with the people who might benefit from it, I am thinking only about the reader.

The flaw in this plan is that we can never truly get inside the head of another person, so we only ever really know ourselves as a reader. Rather than second-guessing what someone else might think or like, our surest path is to learn what we like and learn to trust it or to identify what we need (or needed in the past) and believe that that is enough. If we write the book we wanted but could not find, or a story we would love to read, we already have an audience of one and can expand from there.

For me this is one of the most valuable aspects of having our own *platform*—which is a series of channels through which we can speak directly to our audience. This might include social media accounts, a blog, a podcast, a cohort of students or workshop participants, or a newsletter mailing list. When we have direct access to readers before a book is out in the world, we can get to know them, understand what pains and moves them, get to know the intersection of what they need and what we want to offer. We can survey them and ask them directly about their hopes and dreams, fears and challenges. We can invite opinions and recommendations, and try out some of our ideas.

It is also increasingly the case that publishers approach people directly to author books, which is another reason that your online presence matters. In such a case the publisher would offer the overall idea, but as the author you would still usually have a lot of scope to write the book you want to write.

Many would-be authors are intimidated by the idea of creating a platform, thinking that they have to promote themselves on it all the time, or share too much about their lives. But if you approach it from a position of service, you'll see that it's not actually about you. The opportunity of a free platform and direct access to readers is a huge advantage of writing in the modern world. You might even come to love it.

Personally, I ignore the experts' rules on how often you should post or send newsletters, and I follow my own creative rhythm. When I am deep in writing mode, I rarely engage online, because I need my creative energy focused on the manuscript. But between books I am very active, interacting with my community, offering creative challenges, teaching free short classes, sharing poetry, giving away inspiring books, and getting to know my followers. Although we can never truly know what is going on inside someone else's mind, social media can offer a surprising window into individual lives, and be a useful gauge for taking the temperature of your wider community. It's also fantastic regular writing practice.

It's important to know that some people simply aren't your book people and their opinion matters about as much as whether a stranger likes your new coat. It's the people you are trying to serve who need your attention. Talk to them. Listen to them. Care about them. Find more of them. Invite them to bring their friends. Nurture a community that inspires you too.

Keep serving your people, and your writing will thrive.

If you write one book, you will probably write
more than one.
None of them will change your worth as a human
being or guarantee future happiness.
Write them anyway.

Chapter 11

HARMONIZING

*Being and non-being create
each other.*

DÁODÉJĪNG VERSE 2[1]
(TRANSLATION
STEPHEN MITCHELL)

Describing the annual cycle of nature in her book, *East Wind Melts the Ice*, former geisha Liza Dalby said:

> Philosophically, (the ancient Chinese) believed the phenomenon of changing seasons to be due to the alternating movement of the two underlying essences that give life to the universe—yang and yin. In the Chinese system, half the year was dominated by the yin ethers, half by the yang. It was as if the living universe were slowly breathing a 180-day inhale of yin, followed by an equally long exhale of yang. There is never a point where one force totally excludes the other.[2]

This is a mirror for the rhythm of a writing life underpinned by pairs of coexisting opposite forces: fear and love, shadow and light, chaos and order. *Yin* is associated with the feminine, a passive, receiving energy, and with turning inward. The character for *yin* in Japanese (陰), which is read *in*, means shadow. *Yang* is associated with the masculine, an active, creative energy, and with turning outward. The character for *yang* in Japanese (陽), which is read *yō*, means light.

Yin and yang coexist in our physical environments, in our psyches, and in our writing.

When I reflect on the way we are conditioned to think about creative progress, and how we give so much of our attention to the outside world, there is a clear emphasis on the *yang*. We chase writing targets, we rush projects to completion by a set deadline, we go for the spotlight with metrics-based publishing results. But *yin* success has value too. The grace of receiving inspiration and witnessing it take shape, the nourishment of solitude, and your gentle growth as a writer and human being, are all the results of turning the attention inward.

The writing life is not either/or—it is both. This unity of opposites is one way of describing the elusive *Dao*, or the Way. It is an intelligent rhythm that pulses through life. An eternal flux that we can neither control nor abandon, it is the blood running through the veins of a fearless writing life.

These opposing forces exist in our writing too. If we want to write about freedom, we have to consider what it means to be trapped. To write truth, we must encounter deception. To write fear, we must also write love.

In this chapter we will explore some of the main pairs of coexisting forces that can hinder progress in our writing life if we view only one or other element in isolation, but which will support our progress if we acknowledge and honor their co-existence.

Fear and love

Before *Freedom Seeker* was published, I went along to an event put on by my publisher showcasing talks from several of its authors. Each of them took to the stage for half an hour without notes. I wanted to be on that stage the following year when my book came out, but I felt far from ready, so I decided to take some action to prepare, and signed up for speaker training with a coach named Gail Larsen.[3]

On the first day, Gail asked us what would be a breakthrough. I replied, "To speak for thirty minutes without a script." Even saying it out loud made me feel sick, but I wanted to learn how to tell a story on stage. The workshop began with a series of personal questions, which we took turns answering in pairs. Having heard our responses, our partner had to identify our "original medicine"—the essence of who we truly are—and capture it in the form of a name. That name would then serve as a reminder to show up fully as our true self on stage (and in life). I was given the name Braveheart.

On the final day of the workshop we had to perform our talks to the group. I stayed up late the night before wrestling with the bones of my story, but it just wasn't working. Exhausted, I gave up and went to sleep. The next morning I got up early and went for a run around Santa Fe. The sun was shining, I had good tunes in my ears, and I found myself dancing down the road. Interrupted by traffic at a large crossroads, I carried on dancing on the spot. Two girls across the way were staring at me as if I was odd. Embarrassed, I nearly stopped dancing, but then remembered that I was Braveheart. I countered my fear of ridicule with a sense of joy. As the lights changed we crossed toward each other, me still dancing, them laughing. Then something shifted. They looked at each other, and started to dance too. A couple of minutes later I looked back and they were still dancing far up the street.

My brave heart was pumping out of my body, and I knew that I was ready to give my talk. When it was done, the group cheered and Gail whooped. "Talk about tearing up the f***ing script!" she said.

Reflecting on what had happened I realized that where there had been fear, there had also been love, and this holds true in writing and in life. Being a fearless writer means having a brave heart. Having a brave heart means acknowledging both fear and love, knowing that they are always giving rise to each other. Fear contains within it the seed of love. Love contains within it the seed of fear. The secret of fearless writing is acknowledging and accepting that fear and love exist in relationship to each other.

Fearless writing is not writing in the absence of fear but writing in the presence of love.

By focusing only on the fear, we get stuck. By recognizing that love must also be present, we free ourselves to write from our brave hearts.

Shadow and light

Many years ago I wangled a month off university to interpret for the British Bobsleigh Team at the 1998 Winter Olympic Games in Japan. On a rest day between training runs and the main competition, a group of us snuck into Nagano to visit Zenkōji, a temple famous for the legend of a secret underground passage. We followed a priest up Chūō-dōri, past street stalls and Olympic pin-badge swap shops, to the seventh-century temple, which lies at the heart of the modern city. We found the staircase and descended into darkness, feeling our way along 100 meters of wall in an attempt to find the "Key to Paradise," which is said to be hidden in the tunnel and would, apparently, offer us salvation.

Writing both the shadow and the light makes our words more real and relatable.

I didn't find the key, but I did experience an extraordinary meditation on absolute darkness, emerging from the tunnel with a floating sensation, as if my brain had been through a car wash. As we stood squinting in the harsh light of a sky ready to snow, I realized that we hardly ever experience absolute darkness, just as pure brightness is rare. Instead, shadow and light coexist all around.

In his classic treatise on Japanese aesthetics, *In Praise of Shadows*, novelist Junichirō Tanizaki argued that an awareness of beauty is essential for a well-lived life, and that such beauty can be found anywhere, even in dark places. Speaking of temple architecture he said,

> And surely you have seen, in the darkness of the innermost rooms of these huge buildings, to which sunlight never penetrates, how the gold leaf of a sliding door or screen will pick up a distant glimmer from the garden, then suddenly send forth an ethereal glow, a faint golden light cast into the enveloping darkness, like the glow upon the horizon at sunset. In no other setting is gold quite so exquisitely beautiful.[4]

Sometimes there is only a glimmer of joy, or hope, in the dark places we write about. Sometimes a hint of darkness or difficulty can make a joyous piece of writing seem more relatable.

*

Together shadow and light symbolize transformation, which is an essential part of any story, and the defining characteristic of a writing life. As writers, we cannot be changed without being called to write about it. And as writers, we cannot write without being changed.

WRITE NOW #41

In your notebook draw two vertical lines to divide your page into three columns.

In column 1 write short descriptions of five people, each with an accessory.

In column 2 write five words that represent moods you think of when you hear the word "darkness."

In column 3 write five words that represent environments or places you think of when you hear the word "darkness."

Now pick one item from each column at random and use them as a writing spark, weaving in both shadow and light.

Ebb and flow

There is a beautiful, gentle word at the heart of Japanese culture, known as *chōwa* (調和), meaning harmony or balance, which I believe is essential for a flourishing writing life. Movement and stillness. Spontaneity and routine. Community and solitude. There is a place for each of them.

One action or choice is not better than the other. Rather, they exist in relationship and we need to integrate them, honoring the ebb and flow of our energy, time commitment, interest, and priorities. There are times for patience and times for perseverance, times for doing and times for dreaming, times for action and times for rest.

Sometimes the seasons determine that rhythm for me. I prefer to work on my books through the winter, when the weather is grim and my writing room is cozy. I tend to have a lot of ideas for new projects in spring, and I am happy to turn my energy outward and engage brightly with my community in summer and autumn, which is when my books tend to be published.

In your case, you might prefer to flow with the rhythm of the moon, or with the school year. The work we can do is also affected by what is happening in the world, the state of our health, any personal challenges we face, and the particular **Find a** life stage we are moving through. Having an awareness **rhythm.** of the forces at work in our lives can help us figure out what to prioritize in order to stay well and keep writing.

In my experience of living a creative life with small children and a business to run, I have found that it is extremely difficult to find balance on a single day, but it's absolutely possible to find a rhythm, and harmonize various aspects of life, over a calendar year. Knowing this makes it easier to focus fiercely for short bursts, and get support for that. I can still jump on my paddleboard at short notice if the sun comes out.

WRITE NOW #42

Pick a magazine you love and write a feature for it, on the theme of "rhythm."

Chaos and order

I have been practicing non-attachment for a long time now, but somehow my obsession with stationery always seems to scupper my efforts. It began when I was in primary school, and just a few years shy of fifty I probably should have quit already, but the truth is I get as excited by stationery now as I did back then. These days I have upgraded to a *Hobonichi Techō*, a Japanese diary with a smart vertical layout made with a particularly thin but durable paper originally used for dictionaries. Its week-at-a-glance layout brings order to my days, and it is my secret weapon for getting things done.

Creating is a chaotic experience, and if you are a sensitive soul, which most writers seem to be, trying to do it in a chaotic environment can be overwhelming. If our walls, bookshelves, and surfaces are crowded with stuff, there can be too many sensory inputs, which can affect our creative output. Personally I create much more easily in a calm and tidy space.

The healthy chaos of the creative process is facilitated by healthy order in daily life.

It's the same with my schedule. If it's crowded and chaotic, jumping from one project to another in a single day, I find it hard to go deep in my writing. When a book deadline is approaching, I block out four days a week and only email on Wednesdays. My schedule is more relaxed at other times but still, I tend to block out half or full days for writing. Outside that time I batch tasks as much as possible, and I only email at certain times of day. Even if you have a full-time job, it's important to carve out time for your writing, put it in your calendar and keep it clear, so the chaos of your creativity has a space to fill. Remember, organizing your schedule is as much about managing other people's expectations of when you will be available as it is for your own use.

Every writer works differently, but I'm sure a little order can help anyone. Don't get sucked into the urban myth that real creation only happens in chaos. The creation itself is chaotic, but getting your surroundings and schedule in good order can help you focus on the chaos that matters.

WRITE NOW #43

Describe your writing space, as it is right now.

Remove half the objects you can see, even if you just put them in a box to sort out later.

Make some notes about how you feel in your slightly edited, more orderly space.

Failure and success

If something is so important to us that we have dedicated months or years to writing it, it is natural to want as many people as possible to read it. We took risks and made sacrifices for those words. Our stories mean so much to us. But at the end of it all, we are faced with the harsh reality of sales figures on a royalty statement telling us exactly how many people have bought the book. There's nowhere to hide. The commercial success of a book is just one of myriad measures of "success" in writing, all of which matter in some ways, but none of which have any bearing on your value as a human being. I think we all know that, it's just hard to remember it sometimes.

Scrolling through my own Instagram feed looking for something,

I came across a photo of a kind-looking Japanese man holding a copy of *Wabi Sabi*, taken the year after it was published. The caption said, "This is Mr. Nakatsuyama, a bookseller at Kyōto's Maruzen, a bookshop founded 150 years ago. My homestay father worked there. As a nineteen-year-old language student living in Kyōto, I used to love spending time among the towering shelves dreaming of being able to read the Japanese books, so it was a tiny joy to walk in and find *Wabi Sabi* on the shelf in the English language section on Japanese culture, next to Marie Kondō."

This to me was a win, not because a big bookshop stocked one of my books, but because of what it meant for that particular bookshop to hold it. It was evidence of a personal transformation, from the wide-eyed teenager struggling with a complex language, visiting the shop to buy dictionaries and study materials, to someone who had persevered with those studies long enough that she got to write a book inspired by one of the most elusive words in that same language.

I could have looked at it differently. I could have seen one copy of my book next to ten copies of *The Life-Changing Magic of Tidying Up* and seen failure, comparing my perfectly respectable sales figures to Marie Kondō's ten million–plus sales and coming up short. But here's the thing: when we consider failure and success in terms of our achievements compared with those of other people, it only builds the ego or crushes our confidence, both of which distance us from others and stifle our creativity. When we instead consider failure and success as coexisting forces that can support our growth as human beings, this builds compassion, courage, and confidence, which can bring us closer to others and inspire us to keep going.

External success is not irrelevant in the modern publishing world. If we win awards, or have great reviews, or achieve bestseller status, or if our books keep popping up everywhere as people share them over and over, it can help potential readers to trust us before they know our work. If a book sells well, it's more likely a publisher will want to back the next one. In this way success breeds opportunity, and the likelihood of more success. To ignore this reality is naive. But to become a slave to it is just as dangerous.

The dogged pursuit of this kind of external success can be exhausting—and obstructive to the creative process. When I think about the everyday reality of writing, anything relating to getting exposure for my books tends to be a distraction. There are more emails to respond to, more interviews to prepare for, more promotion to do. Over here my heart is happiest when I am free to sit at my desk, pen in hand, pondering questions of human existence, shaping them into book form, and wrapping them with love in the hope that they will make a difference to someone—or lots of someones.

Look for the successes woven into failure, and be mindful of the failures embedded in success. It can transform the way you feel about things.

Therein lies the challenge. Because to reach lots of someones we have to talk about our work. We have to create our own chances and feed the conversation. Selling books and being paid to write, or being paid for spin-off activities such as teaching and speaking, can buy us more time to write. If we generate enough money from it that we don't have to do another job alongside writing, we have a lot more time and energy for the writing we want to do.

Even though we have spent a lot of time talking about desirelessness, I am not going to tell you that success in the material world will make no difference to your day-to-day experience, because, actually, if it buys you more time to write, it can make a huge difference.

I try to separate the creation of the book itself with the sharing of the book in the world. For me personal success in writing is in no small part about how I get to spend my daily life. The joy of writing is in the satisfaction of finding the words that will say what I really want to say, the astonishing experience of engagement with the mysterious powers of creation, and the intellectual and emotional challenge of laying words onto the page and connecting hearts across continents and cultures.

There is no defined career progression for a writer, which is an anomaly in the modern world. Perhaps we have been looking at it all wrong. Perhaps the lack of a ladder actually gives us freedom from the pressure of rising through the ranks and permission to live an unconventional life doing what we love. To me that's a tremendous success right there.

Ultimately you need to decide what writing success means to you. As you think about this, I encourage you to look beyond material goals and consider all the things writing brings to your life.

WRITE NOW #44

Think back on an experience you have previously considered to be a failure. Which part of it was a success in terms of how you changed as a person, or what happened instead?

Think back on something you consider a success. What failed—or didn't go as you had hoped or expected—along the way, that ended up making the success happen?

Acknowledge the fear.
Look for the love.
Keep writing.

Chapter 12

LIVING

泣いて暮らすも一生、
笑って暮らすも一生
(naite kurasu mo isshō,
waratte kurasu mo isshō)

*Life can be lived in tears or in
laughter, so you might as well live
it in laughter.*

JAPANESE PROVERB

The four noble truths of Buddhism are the truth of suffering, the truth of the origin of suffering, the truth of the end of suffering, and the truth of the path to the end of suffering. Regardless of our faith or beliefs, there is wisdom here for every writing life.

The truth of suffering is that we get old, we get sick, and we die, and along the way our desires and cravings are unsatisfied. Therein lies the source of all the inspiration a writer might ever need.

The truth of the origin of suffering is desire, and the truth of the end of suffering is letting go of that desire. This is why desirelessness is a gate of liberation for the fearless writer.

The truth of the path to the end of suffering is the Eightfold Path of right understanding, right thoughts, right speech, right action, right livelihood, right effort, right mindfulness, and right concentration.[1] These can be gathered into the themes of wisdom, ethical conduct, and meditation, which sound to me like a much healthier guide for a writing life than a fixation on desire.

This doesn't mean that we cannot dream. I have a small hand-bound book covered in pink silk, which I bought from the San Jose Museum of Art a dozen years ago. I was on my way to the art retreat that would inspire me to walk away from my job and found my own business, Do What You Love. At the end of the retreat we were encouraged to make some notes about what we would like to bring to life in the weeks and months that followed, in order to sustain the momentum. I was working in the corporate world back then, and I went all out making lists of goals in my little pink book. There were short-term goals, medium-term goals, and long-term goals. I got very serious about my lists and wrote down a lot of things, most of which seemed completely unrealistic. But I was inspired and excited . . . and then I lost the book.

After I returned to England, life got busy again. I did quit my job and start a business, but as I couldn't remember exactly what I had written down, I never got around to making a detailed plan for making it happen.

Fast-forward a few years and I found the book in a cardboard box in the attic. How it got there, I have no idea. I looked through the lists of goals and gasped. Almost everything had happened. Not in the order that I expected, or within the time frame I had suggested, and sometimes not in the form I had anticipated, but my audacity had paid off.

I call it my "Little Book of Dreams That All Came True" and it reminds me that it's good to dream, and it's good not to try to force those dreams into a certain shape, by a certain time.

When we use our vast imaginations to dream without expect-ation, it can inspire us and encourage us to commit to a particular action, which can open new doors and lead to an expanded life. But if we attach expectations to our dreams, that leads to the dichotomy of success or failure, extremes of elation or disap-pointment, a sense of entitlement, and bitterness if it doesn't go to plan. But as the *Dáodéjīng* teaches, it is in letting go of desire and judgment that we discover what really matters—the universal truths and peace deep within.

Two thousand years ago, Daoist mystics sought freedom, adopting "an unconventional and carefree way of life, living according to nature."[2] This sounds like my kind of flourishing writing life.

WRITE NOW #45

Today, take some time to consider what "a flourishing writing life" means to you. Consider which elements of that you are already living, and what small changes you could make to move even closer toward it. Then make a list of any dreams you have that are related to your writing life. Spend a while on this, then tape up the page, or tear it out, seal it in an envelope, and hide it somewhere safe, to discover at some point in the future.

Let go of the need to force your writing dreams into being in a certain way or by a certain date, and trust that they will come to life in one form or another in good time. The work takes the time

Always go back to writing.

it takes. Building a writing life takes the time it takes. Dream a little, and then go back to writing.

Choose where to focus

Writers tend to have a lot of ideas. One of the questions I am asked most often in my classes is how to know which idea to pursue. Can I let you in on a secret? Besides the two nonfiction books I am currently working on, I have ideas for three novels, a poetry collection, a Christmas movie script, a guided journal, and a series of children's stories. My interest in each of them waxes and wanes. I might suddenly get a flood of inspiration for one of the projects and spill it into a file. Then the intensity passes and something else becomes interesting. If we view this lack of fidelity to a single project as negative, that judgment can lodge in us and we can start to view it as writer's block. But I don't see it like that at all. I am not procrastinating, or being flaky. It simply means the idea isn't yet ready. This marination is a vital part of the process, and we have to cultivate patience in the writing life.

When I look back in my journals, I can see that I first mentioned an idea that would inform *Wabi Sabi* (which was published in 2018) in a journal entry in 2012, and the seeds of *Freedom Seeker* (which was published in 2017) were sown as far back as 2007.

I know that one of the ideas is maturing into a book when it keeps pushing itself forward. No longer is it small flashes of insight here and there. Rather, it becomes the lens through which I see everything else. When I can't stop thinking about it, and I see hints of a need for it everywhere, I know it's ready to pursue. At this stage it is all about the energy of the idea.

Don't write what you think you should write. Write what burns in you. Write what begs to be written. Write what you can't not write before you die.

> ## WRITE NOW #46
>
> Think about all the pieces of yourself that you have given away or exiled over the years. Make a list. Which of these most strongly connects to the themes that come up when you think about writing a book? Write about calling back that part of you.

Learn patience

One of my favorite *yin* yoga poses is pentacle, a variation of śavāsana, where you lie on your back in a starfish shape, waiting without anxiety. This is the opposite of how we usually wait: tensely, expectantly, attached to the hope of a particular outcome.

There is a lot of waiting in writing. We have to wait for the ideas to come, wait for them to take shape, wait for feedback, wait for responses to pitches and proposals, wait to see what readers think. Training myself to wait without anxiety has been a game changer. Even just saying out loud, "I am waiting without anxiety" can help. If it gets really bad, such as when I have sent in a new book proposal, and I find myself refreshing my email every two minutes to see if my agent has responded, I actually get up from my seat and lie on the floor in pentacle pose, breathing slowly. We have to learn to take care of ourselves like this if we want a sustainable writing life. In the West the creation of masterpieces has long been associated with struggle. In the East,

Waiting is a lot less stressful if we learn to wait without anxiety.

the emphasis is on relaxation and enjoyment. If I'm going to be in this for the long haul, I'd rather create from a place of ease and joy. If I feel anxious about my work or can sense resistance, I check to see if I have slipped back into my old ways:

- Have I become attached to a particular desire for this work to be a certain way, or to be connected to a certain kind of success in the material world? Am I trying to control what happens next?
- Am I trying to force the form of the work too soon? Am I giving its form too much attention, editing before the words have hit the page?
- Am I isolating myself or comparing myself to others, getting caught up in the idea of them being separate to me, seeing everyone as judge, competition, and critic? Am I focused on this particular idea as a separate entity, rather than seeing how it is connected to everything else (which can be a tremendous source of inspiration)?

If so, I revisit the three sacred gates, and breathe.

WRITE NOW #47

Look back on your writing journey so far and tell the story of something you once doubted but now know to be true.

Co-creating

"So what do you want to write a song about?" Danni's face beamed out of my laptop. "I'm not sure really. Life. Time. The detail and the vastness. The not knowing. The wanting to know. The not needing to know." Danni Nicholls is a professional singer–songwriter who generously agreed to co-write a song with me, as a fearless writing test. When I began to think about this book, I pondered what would be the most challenging writing experience I could imagine, and that was it. I love music, but I am not musical, so songwriting seemed out of reach, and co-writing sounded even harder, because it would involve spilling unpolished liquid words onto the ground in front of another human being.

"And how do you feel about doing this?" Danni asked.

"I'm terrified," I answered, before I had the time to check in with myself and see how I was really feeling. When I did that I realized that actually, I wasn't terrified at all. I was unsure of how it would work out, so I was a little nervous. I felt vulnerable knowing that I would have no room to edit the words that came out of my mouth before Danni caught them and wove them in with her own. But the overriding feeling was actually one of excitement.

During those three hours of co-writing *The River* with Danni, I had a strange sense that the song was materializing in the space between us, as if our separateness had dissolved at the edges to make room for it. We often talk of writing as a solitary pursuit, but actually, whether our co-creator is a singer–songwriter with Americana vibes or the creative energy of the universe itself, we are never alone in our work.

This reminds me of a commentary on the collaborative Japanese poetry genre, *renga*, in which alternating verses are linked by successive poets. Writing about this poetry form, Kyōto University professor Tadashi Ogawa said:

The work of the fearless writer is to abandon the self and enter into the ocean of a shared life.

The essential basics of *renga* lie in both self-abandonment and the participation in *za*, which is "the opening place" belonging neither to one's self nor to that of the others. In short, what matters most is to abandon the "funk hole" or "dugout" of the self and enter into the ocean of a shared life with others.[3]

This was exactly what we had to do in order to co-write the song, and what we have to do as individual writers in order to co-create with the energy of the universe.

WRITE NOW #48

Write a list of things you don't know. Include wonder as well as worry.

Then, taking inspiration from your list, write a love song.

Express gratitude

At the turn of the millenium I spent the best part of three years working at the 2002 FIFA World Cup in Tōkyō. I was responsible for the accommodation for all national teams playing in Japan, including all the hotels in the venues, and at training camps spread across the country. I had to negotiate millions of dollars' worth of contracts. When I started I was twenty-three. My boss was Mexican and spoke no Japanese. I was one of the first employees in a team that would swell rapidly as the tournament approached, but in those early days, there were only a handful of us, so we got to choose the jobs we wanted. By the time the tournament came to town, I was sleeping about four hours a day and carrying three mobile phones at all times. I suffered from imposter syndrome before I even knew it had a name.

My body can still remember the intense physical feeling of it. I would be standing in the lobby of a swanky five-star hotel, waiting for the arrival of some of the world's most famous footballers, wondering when I would be found out. I remember being in a meeting of a handful of the most powerful people in sport, wondering how I got there. I recall staring at my access-all-areas accreditation pass and the stack of World Cup tickets in my hand, wondering when someone was going to tap me on the shoulder and accuse me of stealing them.

Reverend Kawakami, deputy head priest at five-hundred-year-old Shunkōin Temple in Kyōto, who is regularly invited to speak about Zen and mindfulness in the corporate world, told me that imposter syndrome seems to be one of the most common challenges that executives struggle with today. Many people in power can't believe they are there. The problem, he says, is that we are seeing ourselves as separate from one another. To have imposter syndrome is to believe that you got where you are on your own merits and effort alone, and to doubt that your experience and expertise justifies your position. But when we remember that we are actually all connected, and that everything we do, or accomplish, is thanks to the interconnected web of everything and everyone who has gone before, we stop seeing our achievements as ours alone, which makes them much more likely. The burden of success does not just belong to us.

With nonfiction in particular, when you write a book you are putting yourself forward as some kind of expert. To say that you are the only person in the world who can write that book that way is at once completely true—and completely intimidating. A book brings with it a particular flavor of self-doubt, because it is such a huge and public project. I find that it helps to take a moment to acknowledge those who have helped us to get in a position where we can write the book, because it keeps us humble, and it reminds us that we are not alone in this endeavor. Other people, all our life experiences and the universe itself, contribute to what we are able to write at any given moment.

This is a fine time to pause and honor those who have helped us to get this far. Our writing is informed by everything that has gone before, everything we have read, watched, heard, and experienced, everything we have been taught, every conversation we have had, and everything that has broken or opened our hearts.

It's also a good time to take a moment to articulate our gratitude for writing itself. Thanks to writing, I've found meaning for my curiosity and got to explore what it means to be human and to call that work. Thanks to writing, I have experienced it snowing inside a room, had afternoon tea with a Cirque du Soleil clown, and had conversations with my literary heroes. Thanks to writing, I have taught my daughters what it means to create something from your head and heart, and to turn it into food on the table. I have felt inspired. I have felt useful. I have felt alive.

Thanks to writing, I have learned how to see. Thanks to writing, I have set myself free.

WRITE NOW #49

Make a list of all the ways you are grateful to writing. What has it brought to your life? And who has helped you get here? If they are alive, tell them. If not, find a way to honor them.

Guideposts for a flourishing writing life

Just as no one can tell us how to be human, no one can tell us how to be a writer. There might be rules for writing, but there are no fixed rules for a writing life. Even so, here are some guideposts that might help you on your way from here:

1. Create a sacred writing space and go there often.
2. Write. Write some more. If in doubt, move your body, then write again.
3. Practice writing simply to become more awake. It will change your life.
4. Carry a notebook and pen everywhere.
5. Look with an open mind. Write with an open heart.
6. Be disciplined enough to stay at your desk when you need to, but remember that much of life isn't visible from behind a desk.
7. Have a plan if it makes you feel better, but whatever you do don't stick to the plan.
8. Be kind: to yourself, to other writers, and to your writing.
9. Know that people who don't live the writing life might think that you are weird. That's OK. We're all weird really.
10. Remove everything that is not essential.

11. Know that nothing is ever really finished but that there is such a thing as "done enough."
12. In the beginning, only your opinion matters. In the end only your opinion matters.
13. Everything is connected. Watch closely.
14. Everything changes. Let go.
15. Remember, your writing life is what you make it.

WRITE NOW #50

What is rising in you? Write for ten minutes.

What is falling away? Write for ten minutes.

Make your own set of guideposts to support this next phase of your writing life, where you attend to what is rising in you, and let go of what is falling away.

Know this:
You are a fearless writer,
and the world needs your medicine.

Ceremony at the Third Gate

Take a moment to pause and look around you. We are here at the Gate of Emptiness. We made it. I don't know about you, but I feel quite emotional.

On the path to here we have learned to see the world through *haiku* eyes: just as it is.

We have recognized the impermanence of everything. We have seen this as an infinite source of inspiration and a reminder that all situations pass, and we must keep writing, whatever happens.

We have learned how words can coalesce to become a book, and how a book can make a difference.

We have learned not to attach our self-worth and future happiness to our writing in a cause-and-effect linear way, but rather to see writing and life as interwoven paths of growth.

We have come to understand that writing fearlessly does not mean writing without fear, but writing in the presence of the love which always coexists with that fear.

We have come to know that we are not alone, and that everything is connected.

I am so proud of you—so proud of us. For shedding our conditioning and finding our way: the Way of the Fearless Writer.

As we cross the threshold of the Gate of Emptiness, I invite you to speak these words out loud:

I am here.
I am grateful.
I am fearlessly living the writing life.

I hope you will carry this blessing with you as you venture onward:

May you know that the work of the fearless writer
is to see into the heart of being,
to give voice to pain,
to celebrate wonder,
and to stay aware of your connection to everything.
May you show compassion to yourself,
to other writers,
and to your readers
through the words you offer to them.
May the light of creation
brighten your own spirit,
and help you to offer hope
to those in darkness.
May you continue to tell
of the remarkable and unremarkable
which make this life,
and see beauty in the ordinary
every single day.

Come now my friend, the time has come.

Step through this final gate,
and onward,
into your flourishing writing life.

Journey Note 4

Beyond the Gates

My recollection of that summer night is hazy. Mr. K and I had cycled to a friend's home for dinner at the foot of the Higashiyama mountains in Kyōto. Hiroko's husband, a philosophy professor, had plied us with too much good wine, and somehow we had leaped from tales of their old life in London to the subject of the lotus as a symbol of spiritual growth, purity, and enlightenment. They told us about a quiet garden in the grounds of Nanzenji Temple, just around the corner from their house, where lotus flowers bloom. Mr. K had never been to Nanzenji, and we all thought that it would be a good idea to go there immediately, even though it was dark now, the temple was closed, and the lotus flowers were sleeping.

I hadn't thought about that night, some ten years ago, until a postcard arrived from Hiroko recently, bearing a picture of the Sanmon, the great gate at the entrance to Nanzenji. And then it all came flooding back: how the professor had told us that the word *sanmon* (三門), literally "three gates," refers to the Three Gates of Liberation in Buddhism. Now, looking again at the imposing wooden entrance gate built some four centuries ago, instead of seeing the structure itself, I see the negative space: the three rectangular entrances adjacent to each other within the gate. And then it dawns on me. The Three Gates of Liberation don't follow one another on a linear path; they stand alongside each other at the symbolic threshold between the mundane and the sacred.

The fearless writing path is actually a pathless path, unfolding with each step and leading us not from here to there, but from here to here. It is a path of waking up. Our work as fearless writers is to pass through these three gates over and over, every time we enter our sacred writing space. Shedding our fixed identity. Letting go of our desire and our need for control. Honoring the formlessness of our creative potential. Sensing the interconnectedness of everything. And practicing. Always practicing, to express the human condition and this strange and beautiful experience of existence, in words.

Life happens, things change. We get pulled back toward desire, and form, and separateness, and we have to keep recommitting to what will free us: desirelessness, formlessness, emptiness. As writers we have to do the impossible. We have to travel through all three gates at once, like some kind of strange quantum physics experiment on the nature of reality.

The gates have no doors. They are symbolic. There is nothing stopping us from passing through. We just have to keep showing up with courage, humility, and grace as we cross the threshold between the mundane and the sacred every single time we choose to write, never quite knowing what will happen next.

There is a beautiful four-hundred-year-old *haiku* by Matsuo Bashō that captures how I want my writing life to be. It speaks of a cicada shell, and the cicada that sang itself utterly away. I want to write myself utterly away, not just once like the cicada but over and over. When we dissolve our edges and limitations, we are free to wander wherever we please, exploring all words can do, and all we can be. We can travel in any direction: north, south, east or west, inward or outward, into the past or future, or deeply into the present, and we can bring back what we find there, often surprising ourselves with its beauty, vitality, and resonance.

I hope you will remember this, and stay open, surrendering to the creations that want to be born through you. I hope that you will see the magnificence in your own ordinariness and the ordinariness in your own magnificence.

As the old Buddhist saying goes: *esha jyōri* (会者定離), parting is inevitable. We meet all sorts of people on the writing road, and I am grateful to have met you. We must soon part, but I'm sure we will meet again. As the pearl-diving *ama* said, "This is a job without beginning or end," and writing friends are never far away. I wish you a long and flourishing writing life.

Go now, and write yourself utterly away.

Epilogue

Sunlight is reaching through the tall stone windows of Gladstone's Library in Wales, spilling a tin of gold paint over the stacks of old books. Xavier Rudd's "Follow the Sun" is pouring into my headphones, taking me back to Costa Rica and the eagle, and the moment after which everything was different.

I am in the mysticism section of the library, and I pull down a book at random from the shelf next to me. Out flies a paper bird. It swoops down to the reading room below, then back up to the vaulted ceiling to join with thousands of others in a silent murmuration.

My heart swells to meet the birds, and I can feel the moment expanding. I scan the walls and wonder how the world has room for any more books, and I know that we must never stop writing books.

I look up again and the birds have become tiny blank pages, floating down gently like paper snow, covering everything.

I pick up my pen to write once more, joining the lineage of all other humans who have been awake to the world and written about it. And suddenly the strange happenings in that bookshop in Beijing all those years ago make sense.

On the surface, the bookshop was simply an unusual stationery store selling leather-bound journals. The *kōan* was not the shop itself, but the naming of the blank volume as the *Dáodéjīng,* one of the most famous books in the world. *Kōans* are not so much riddles to be solved, as paradoxical phrases to be contemplated, in a way that allows the mind to transcend logic and see beyond.

The truth revealed in that strange old shop in Beijing on that dark rainy night years ago was this:

> An empty book holds the potential of everything.
> The blank page is a symbol of life in any given moment.
> Every page is a new day,
> Every word a new beginning,
> Every beginning seeded in the ending of all that
> went before.
> We don't have to be able to explain things to write them,
> And yet in writing them we somehow come to know them.
> All we have to do is pick up a pen.

Just as the *Dáodéjīng* tells us that the *Dáo* that can be spoken is not the Dáo,[1] the Way of the Fearless Writer that can be fully articulated is not the Way. But we know now that it is deeply intertwined with our experience of the great unfolding, and the endless flow of life as creative beings who use language to express ourselves, reach others, and reinforce the interconnected web of everything. And just as the Dao represents the creative process of the universe, the Way of the Fearless Writer—the journey toward the three gates of liberation—represents the creative process of becoming who we really are, and the freedom found in spilling our words onto the page.

> All that can be said has been said.
> All that is left cannot be said.
> All there is left to do is to write.

Acknowledgments

The books we write are intimately connected to all the other books in the world—the ones we have read, the ones that inspired the authors of those books, the ones our readers have read that set them on a trail to discover ours, and so on. I am grateful to the author of each one, and to every translator whose work has illuminated ideas from long ago and far away.

People often say that writing is a lonely task, but when I turn and look back at the path I have walked, I see the footprints of so many people I am grateful for. Some are still right here alongside me now, and I know there will be others up ahead. To each of you, including my writerly friends, thank you. Specifically, though, I would like to honor my teachers, in particular Naomi Cross, William McClure, Dr. John Weste, Ariko Komiya, Yūko Nakajima, Kaori Nishizawa, Junko Suzuki, Julia Tuff, Roshi Joan Halifax, Kazuaki Tanahashi, and the faculty of the Upaya Zen Center, Darin Lehman, Lacey Hickox Lehman, Srimati Hughes, Sam Bianchini, Hana Pepin, Angie Howell, Yūko Kubota, Dr. Martin Shaw, Mark Nepo, Horatio Clare, and the late Joy Sander.

Behind the scenes of every book there is a team of people who work to get that book out in the world. I am so grateful to my wonderful agent Caroline Hardman of Hardman & Swainson, and to the brilliant Thérèse Coen for doing the deals that have seen my books translated into more than twenty-five languages. It's more than I ever dreamed of. I am blessed to work with my fantastic editor Jillian Young, and am grateful to all at Piatkus who have helped bring this book to life and get it out in the world, particularly Jillian Stewart, Jan Cutler, Matthew Burne, and Matt Crossey.

I am deeply indebted to Don Starr, Director of Studies (Chinese and Japanese) at the University of Durham, for advice on the *Dáodéjīng* and the use of Chinese, and to Seiko Mabuchi, Audrey Flett, Teruyuki Kuchū, Craig Anczelowitz, and Reverend Takafumi Kawakami for invaluable advice and guidance on the Japanese references in this book. Any errors or omissions are my responsibility.

To all my students, thank you for showing me that what I had to say about writing was worth writing down.

To all the booksellers, librarians, and readers who have so generously recommended my books to others, and taken the time to let me know how much they have meant to you, thank you. It makes such a difference.

Writing books requires intense periods of time away from other commitments. I am especially grateful to our business partners Lilla Rogers and Rachael Taylor, and to our team, for your ongoing support, and for doing what you do so well. Thank you also to Kelly Rae Roberts for the reminder that nothing is wasted, Kate Eckman for the name "Braveheart," Bill and Joanna for the cottage, and Finn for all the coffee.

I am indebted to my mum for filling my childhood with books, supporting my endless projects, and always encouraging me to write, and to my dad for lending me your typewriter (and all your pens) and bravely sharing your own words first.

And, of course, to Mr. K and our girls, Sienna and Maia: thank you for helping me build a hermitage, and filling life outside it with love and laughter. I love your stories best of all.

Finally, I offer my eternal gratitude to the universe, co-author of everything I have ever written.

Bibliography

Bhavabhuti (trans. Schelling, Andrew), Untitled Poem in *Dropping the Bow: Poems of Ancient India* (New York: White Pine Press, 2008).

Dalby, Liza, *East Wind Melts the Ice: A Memoir through the Seasons* (London: Chatto & Windus, 2007).

Ehrlich, Gretel, *Facing the Wave: A Journey in the Wake of the Tsunami* (New York: Vintage, 2013).

Farhi, Donna, *The Breathing Book* (New York: St. Martin's Griffin, 1996).

Gogen Yurai (online etymological dictionary), https://gogen-yurai.jp/omoshiroi/. Retrieved March 1, 2022.

Halpern, Jack (ed.), *The Kodansha Kanji Dictionary* (New York: Kodansha USA, 2013).

Hanh, Thich Nhat, *Awakening of the Heart: Essential Buddhist Sutras and Commentaries* (Berkeley: Parallax Press, 2012).

Hass, Robert, *The Essential Haiku: Versions of Bashō, Buson & Issa* (Northumberland: Bloodaxe, 2013).

Higginson, William J. and Harter, Penny, *The Haiku Handbook: How to Write, Teach, and Appreciate Haiku* (New York: Kodansha USA, 2013).

Ishiguro, Kazuo, Nobel Lecture, https://www.nobelprize

.org/prizes/literature/2017/ishiguro/lecture/. Retrieved March 29, 2022.

Japan Ministry of the Environment, *Nokoshitai nihon no onfūkei hyaku sen,* https://www.env.go.jp/air/life/nihon_no_oto/. Retrieved March 7, 2022.

Kano, Jigorō, *The Best Use of Energy, Taisei,* vol.1, no.1, 1922, http://kodokanjudoinstitute.org/en/doctrine/word/seiryoku-zenyo/. Retrieved February 18, 2022.

Katagiri, Dainin, *The Light That Shines Through Infinity: Zen and the Energy of Life* (Boulder: Shambhala, 2017).

Lao Tzu (trans. Addiss, Stephen and Lombardo, Stanley), *Tao Te Ching* (Indianapolis: Hackett, 1993).

Lao Tzu (trans. Lau D. C.), *Tao Te Ching* (London: Penguin, 1963).

Lao Tzu (trans. Le Guin, Ursula K. with Seaton, J.P.), *Tao Te Ching: A Book About the Way and the Power of the Way* (Boulder: Shambhala, 1997).

Lao Tzu (trans. Mitchell, Stephen), *Tao Te Ching* (London: Frances Lincoln, 2015).

Matsuo, Bashō (trans. Hamill, Sam) *Narrow Road to the Interior* (Boston & London: Shambhala, 1991).

Nakamura, Hiroshi, *Ribbon Chapel,* https://www.nakam.info/en/works/ribbon-chapel/. Retrieved March 8, 2022.

Ogawa, Tadashi. *A Short Study of Japanese RENGA: The Trans-Subjective Creation of Poetic Atmosphere* referenced in Marinucci, Lorenzo, *Hibiki and Nioi: A Study of Resonance in Japanese Aesthetics* http://journals.mimesisedizioni.it/index.php/studi-di-estetica/article/view/879. Retrieved February 11, 2022.

Okumura, Shōhaku, *The Mountains and Waters Sutra: A Practitioner's Guide to Dōgen's Sansuikyō* (Somerville: Wisdom, 2018).

Oxford Languages https://languages.oup.com/google-dictionary
-en/. Retrieved March 13, 2022.

Pike, K. L. and Brend, R. M., *Language as Particle, Wave, and Field*
(1972), https://www.semanticscholar.org/paper/LANGUAGE
-AS-PARTICLE%2C-WAVE%2C-AND-FIELD-Pike
-Brend/7447b4ba7c2eb974b9eb8be6a4d74c5a0158209b.
Retrieved January 15, 2022.

Reps, Paul (ed.), *Zen Flesh, Zen Bones: A Collection of Zen and Pre-
Zen writings* (London: Penguin, 1957).

Schelling, Andrew (trans.), *Dropping the Bow: Poems of Ancient
India* (New York: White Pine Press, 2008).

Shinmura Izuru (ed.) *Kōjien: Dai 5 han* (Tōkyō: Iwanami
Shoten, 1998).

Smith, D. Howard, *The Wisdom of the Taoist Mystics* (London:
Sheldon Press, 1980).

Tanahashi, Kazuaki, *Brush Mind* (Berkeley: Parallax Press, 1998).

Tanahashi, Kazuaki, *Sky Above Great Wind: The Life and Poetry of
Zen Master Ryokan* (Boulder: Shambhala, 2012).

Tanahashi Kazuaki (ed.), *Treasury of the True Dharma Eye: Zen
Master Dogen's Shobo Genzo* (Boulder: Shambhala, 2010).

Tanizaki, Junichirō, (trans. Harper T.J. and Seidensticker E.G.) *In
Praise of Shadows* (London: Vintage, 2001).

Uchiyama, Kōshō, *How to Cook Your Life: From the Zen Kitchen to
Enlightenment* (Boulder: Shambhala, 2005).

United Nations University, *Where the Sea Whistle Echoes,* https://
www.YouTube.com/watch?v=sTIf2vA-_JQ. Accessed
March 6, 2022.

Watts, Alan, with Chung-Liang Huang, Al, *Tao: The Watercourse
Way* (London: Souvenir Press, 2019).

Yoshida, Kenkō (trans. Keene, Donald), *Essays in Idleness
(Tsurezuregusa)* (New York: Columbia University Press, 1967).

Resources for Writers

Writing and storytelling courses
Writing courses with me *dowhatyouloveforlife.com*
National Centre for Writing *nationalcentreforwriting.org.uk*
Curtis Brown Creative *curtisbrowncreative.co.uk*
The Novelry *thenovelry.com*
The School of Myth *schoolofmyth.com*

Writing communities
Live Writing Hour with me *dowhatyouloveforlife.com*
London Writers' Salon *londonwriterssalon.com*
Jericho Writers *jerichowriters.com*
Hope*Writers *hopewriters.com*
She Writes *shewrites.com*
Mslexia *mslexia.co.uk*

Writing retreats
Writing retreats with me *dowhatyouloveforlife.com*
Arvon *arvon.org*
Moniack Mhor *moniackmhor.org.uk*
Hedgebrook *hedgebrook.org*
Unplugged *unplugged.rest*

Podcasts

Beautiful Writers Podcast with Linda Sivertsen

Courage & Spice with Sas Petherick

From My Kitchen Table with Jo Packham

In Writing with Hattie Crisell

Not Too Busy to Write with Penny Wincer and Ali Millar

On Writing with Joshua Pomare

Practice You with Elena Brower

The Creative Penn Podcast with Joanna Penn

The Creative Superheroes Podcast with Andrea Scher

The Good Life Project with Jonathan Fields

The Honest Authors Podcast with Gillian McAllister and
     Holly Seddon

The Rebel Author with Sacha Black

The Secret Life of Writers with Jemma Birrell

The Tim Ferriss Podcast with Tim Ferriss

The Writer Files with Kelton Reid

The Writers Jam with Brad King

The Writing Life from the National Centre for Writing

Windowsill Chats with Margo Tantau

Write Now with Sarah Rhea Werner

Write Now with Scrivener

Write-Minded with Brooke Warner and Grant Faulkner

Writer's Routine with Dan Simpson

References

Journey Note 1

1. Yoshida, Kenkō (trans. Keene, Donald), *Essays in Idleness (Tsurezuregusa)* (New York: Columbia University Press, 1967), p.91.
2. Halpern, Jack (ed.), *The Kodansha Kanji Dictionary* (New York: Kodansha USA, 2013), p. 1560.
3. Ohnishi S.T. and Ohnishi T., *Philosophy, Psychology, Physics and Practice of Ki*, www.ncbi.nlm.nih.gov/pmc/articles/PMC2686635/. Retrieved February 16, 2022.

Chapter 1

1. Lao Tzu (trans. Addiss, Stephen and Lombardo, Stanley), *Tao Te Ching* (Indianapolis: Hackett, 1993), verse 64, no page number available.
2. Lao Tzu (trans. Mitchell, Stephen), *Tao Te Ching* (London: Frances Lincoln, 2015), verse 63, no page number available.
3. Tanahashi, Kazuaki, *Sky Above Great Wind: The Life and Poetry of Zen Master Ryokan* (Boulder: Shambhala, 2012), p. 140.
4. Kano, Jigoro, *The Best Use of Energy, Taisei*, vol.1, no.1, 1922, http://kodokanjudoinstitute.org/en/doctrine/word/seiryoku-zenyo/. Retrieved February 18, 2022.

Chapter 2

1. Tanahashi, Kazuaki, *Brush Mind* (Berkeley: Parallax Press, 1998), p. 61.

2. Farhi, Donna, *The Breathing Book* (New York: St. Martin's Griffin, 1996), p. 5.

Chapter 3

1. Oxford Languages, https://languages.oup.com/google-dictionary -en/. Retrieved March 13, 2022.
2. Gogen Yurai (online etymological dictionary), https://gogen -yurai.jp/omoshiroi/. Retrieved March 1, 2022.

Journey Note 2

1. Watts, Alan, *Tao: The Watercourse Way* (London: Souvenir Press, 2019), p. 55.
2. Ehrlich, Gretel, *Facing the Wave: Journey in the Wake of the Tsunami* (New York: Vintage, 2013), p. 39.

Chapter 5

1. Lao Tzu (trans. Le Guin, Ursula K. with Seaton, J.P.) *Tao Te Ching: A Book About the Way and the Power of the Way* (Boulder: Shambhala, 1997), p. 27.

Chapter 6

1. Lao Tzu (trans. Addiss, Stephen and Lombardo, Stanley), *Tao Te Ching* (Indianapolis: Hackett, 1993), verse 8, no page number available.
2. Japan Ministry of the Environment, *Nokoshitai nihon no onfūkei hyaku sen* https://www.env.go.jp/air/life/nihon_no_oto/. Retrieved February 1, 2022.
3. United Nations University, *Where the Sea Whistle Echoes* https:// www.youtube.com/watch?v=sTIf2vA-_JQ. Retrieved February 1, 2022.
4. See awagami.com.
5. See https://wellcomecollection.org/exhibitions /YLjGYhAAACMAed2Z.
6. Okumura, Shohaku, *The Mountains and Waters Sutra A Practitioner's Guide to Dōgen's Sansuikyō* (Somerville: Wisdom, 2018), p. 24.

7. Lao Tzu (trans. Mitchell, Stephen), *Tao Te Ching* (London: Frances Lincoln, 2015), verse 70, no page number available.

Chapter 7

1. Lao Tzu (trans. Mitchell, Stephen), *Tao Te Ching* (London: Frances Lincoln, 2015), verse 48, no page number available. Note: the original uses "Tao" instead of "Dao," but I have taken the liberty of changing it for consistency.
2. Pike, K.L. and Brend, R.M., *Language as Particle, Wave, and Field* (1972) https://www.semanticscholar.org/paper/LANGUAGE-AS-PARTICLE%2C-WAVE%2C-AND-FIELD-Pike-Brend/7447b4ba7c2eb974b9eb8be6a4d74c5a0158209b. Retrieved January 15, 2022.
3. In this book names of contemporary Japanese people have been given in the format commonly used nowadays, e.g. first name, last name; however, historical names such as Yosa Buson and Matsuo Bashō are given with the surname first. These historical figures are commonly known simply by their first name, i.e. Buson and Bashō.
4. Original haiku by Yosa Buson 遅き日の積もりて遠き昔かな (*osoki hi no / tsumorite tōki / mukashi kana*)—*Long, lazy spring days / piling up— so distant now / the past* (translation my own).
5. Bhavabhuti (trans. Schelling, Andrew), Untitled Poem in *Dropping the Bow: Poems of Ancient India* (New York: White Pine Press, 2008).

Chapter 8

1. Ishiguro, Kazuo, Nobel Lecture, https://www.nobelprize.org/prizes/literature/2017/ishiguro/lecture/. Retrieved March 29, 2022.

Journey Note 3

1. Original haiku by Matsuo Bashō 閑かさや / 岩にしみ入る / 蝉の声 (*shizukasa ya / iwa ni shimi-iru / semi no koe*).
2. Matsuo, Bashō (trans. Hamill, Sam) *Narrow Road to the Interior* (Boston & London: Shambhala, 1991), p. 58.
3. Halpern, Jack (ed.), *The Kodansha Kanji Dictionary* (New York: Kodansha USA, 2013), p. 2767.

4. Shinmura Izuru (ed.) *Kōjien: Dai 5 han* (Tōkyō: Iwanami Shoten, 1998), p. 743.
5. Hanh, Thich Nhat, *Awakening of the Heart: Essential Buddhist Sutras and Commentaries* (Berkeley: Parallax Press, 2012), p. 413.
6. Lao Tzu (trans. Mitchell, Stephen), *Tao Te Ching* (London: Frances Lincoln, 2015), verse 52, no page number available. The original uses "Tao," but I have taken the liberty of replacing this with "Dao" for consistency.
7. Katagiri, Dainin, *The Light That Shines Through Infinity: Zen and the Energy of Life* (Boulder: Shambhala, 2017), p. 142.

Chapter 9

1. Reps, Paul (ed.), *Zen Flesh, Zen Bones: A Collection of Zen and Pre-Zen Writings* (London: Penguin, 1957), p. 43.
2. Uchiyama, Kōshō, *How to Cook Your Life: From the Zen Kitchen to Enlightenment* (Boulder: Shambhala, 2005), p. 66.
3. Foreword by Jane Reichhold in Higginson, William J., and Harter, Penny, *The Haiku Handbook: How to Write, Teach, and Appreciate Haiku* (New York: Kodansha USA, 2013), p. x.
4. You can find a list of traditional Japanese season words here: https://en.wikipedia.org/wiki/List_of_kigo.
5. Original haiku by Matsuo Bashō: 牡丹蘂深く分け出る蜂の名残かな (*botanshibe fukaku wakeizuru hachi no nagori kana*). Translation from Hass, Robert, *The Essential Haiku: Versions of Bashō, Buson & Issa* (Northumberland: Bloodaxe, 2013), p. 34.

Chapter 10

1. See https://www.nakam.info/en/works/ribbon-chapel/.
2. See dowhatyouloveforlife.com.

Chapter 11

1. Lao Tzu (trans. Mitchell, Stephen), *Tao Te Ching* (London: Frances Lincoln, 2015), verse 2, no page number available.
2. Dalby, Liza, *East Wind Melts the Ice: A Memoir Through the Seasons* (London: Chatto & Windus, 2007), p. xxii.

3. You can find Gail at realspeaking.com.
4. Tanizaki, Junichirō (trans. Harper T.J. and Seidensticker E.G.) *In Praise of Shadows* (London: Vintage, 2001), p. 35.

Chapter 12

1. Tanahashi Kazuaki (ed.), *Treasury of the True Dharma Eye: Zen Master Dogen's Shobo Genzo* (Boulder: Shambhala, 2010), p. 1085.
2. Smith, D. Howard, *The Wisdom of the Taoist Mystics* (London: Sheldon Press, 1980), p. 23.
3. Ogawa, Tadashi. *A Short Study of Japanese RENGA: The Trans-Subjective Creation of Poetic Atmosphere* referenced in Marinucci, Lorenzo, *Hibiki and Nioi: A Study of Resonance in Japanese Aesthetics* http://journals.mimesisedizioni.it/index.php/studi-di-estetica/article/view/879. Retrieved February 11, 2022.

Epilogue

1. Lao Tzu (trans. Lau D. C.), *Tao Te Ching* (London: Penguin, 1963), p. 5 (Book 1 Chapter 1).

Index

Note: page numbers in *italics* refer to information contained in tables.

physical/tangible 92
and solid-state writing *98*
formlessness 221
giving shape to 116, 132
value of 11
Formlessness, The Gate of
(*Musōmon*) 11, 85–94
ceremony at the 152–3
toward the 86–94
free-diving 109–10
freedom 40–1, 102
fearless writing as form
of 40
formless sense of 22
Fujimori family 111
Fujiwara, Kōichi 86–8
future
dreams of the 206–8
rush toward 23–4

gardening 48–50
gaseous-state writing 90–2,
97, *98–9*, 99–100, 103,
105–7
Gate of Desirelessness, The
see Muganmon
Gate of Emptiness, The *see
Kūmon*
Gate of Formlessness, The *see
Musōmon*
gates
symbolism of 12
see also Three Gates of
Liberation
Geneva 101
giving up 10

Gladstone's Library, Wales
223
goals 23–4, 57–8, 177, 206–8
Gogen Yurai (etymological
dictionary) 59
gratitude, expression 212–15
grief 50
grounding techniques 48–9
guilt, parental 36

haiku 166–9, 217, 221–2
Haiku Method 178
harmonizing 190–203
and chaos and order 198–9
and ebb and flow 196–7
and failure and success
199–202
and fear and love 193–4
and shadow and light
194–6
healing, through writing
47–8
heart, writing from the 119
Higashiyama mountains,
Kyōto 220
human condition, expression
of the 30–1, 71, 82, 221
human experience, giving
form to 132

ideas 13, 161, 210
cultivation 184
distillation 181
focusing 208–9
generation 182
giving shape to 116

Bonus Q&A with Beth Kempton

Where do you do your best writing?
In nature. I spend a huge part of my writing time out walking, taking a question with me, and scribbling notes or emailing thoughts to myself as I go along. Sometimes I walk by the sea, sometimes I follow a river or take a stroll in the woods.

Are you a morning person or evening person?
I used to tell myself I wasn't a morning person. For years I would stay up until the early hours of the morning studying or working, and have to be dragged out of bed for breakfast. But then I discovered that there is a particular energy in the early hours that is very conducive to writing, and these days it's my favourite time of day. I love my five a.m. writing practice. There is something sacred about getting up while it is still dark, lighting a candle, and writing while you are still caught in that liminal space between sleep and wakefulness. All sorts of things come out.

What is the most important element in your creative practice?
The most important element is questioning. Everything begins with a question for me. Every book is a search for an answer, as

is much of life. The second most important element is solitude, which can be hard to find in a noisy world, but is essential.

What led you to writing this book?
I have been blessed with the experience of teaching writing online to more than thirty thousand people, and I kept seeing the same challenges arising over and over. People are terrified of writing, for lots of reasons but mostly because they are afraid of how they will be judged, even before they have written anything down. I wanted to help them become fearless writers who recognise that their words can be medicine, for themselves and for the world.

What are the primary takeaways you would like readers to draw from the book?
Writing can be as simple as breathe, write, repeat. That's how books are written, poetry is formed, hearts healed, whole worlds imagined. I also hope readers come to see themselves as writers, appreciating that being a writer is no more and no less than capturing things that spill from your head and heart, and putting them on paper, expressing the human condition and experience of existence in words.

Who are some of your favorite authors and how has their work inspired you?
I love writers and poets whose work prompts me to ask big questions about life, and those whose words pierce my heart and make me reread their sentences over and over. Favorites include Jane Hirshfield, Mark Nepo, Dainin Katagiri, Verlyn Klinkenborg, Robert M. Pirsig, Maya Angelou, Eihei Dōgen, Ryōkan Taigu, Matsuo Bashō, Beth Kephart, Arundhati Roy, Victoria Erickson, and Dani Shapiro.

What do you do personally when you hit a writing block?
I have come to understand that a writing block is simply an energy block, so I do something to shift the energy. I go for a walk, do some mindful breathing or meditation, stretch or do some yoga, sing loudly or dance around my kitchen. Sometimes I pull an oracle card, sometimes I talk it out with my husband. Other times I make a cup of tea, then come back and write about something else.

What are some common writer habits you feel are unhelpful?
Wanting to write perfect sentences and getting frustrated when rubbish comes out. Getting fixated on only writing in certain places, with certain pens, in certain conditions. Spending longer talking about writing than actually writing. Waiting until . . . (fill in the blank—they have more time, more money, the perfect partner, a different job, etc.) rather than just writing today.

Is there one piece of advice—about writing, about creativity, about life—you wish you'd been given earlier in your career?
Perfection is a myth. To be human is to be imperfect. Get over it, embrace it, write about it. It will be a huge relief. Also, you have something worth saying. Write it down. Lots of what you write will be rubbish. Some of it will be genius. You have to write a lot to figure out the difference and discover the gems.

How can writing benefit us?
Writing can be a joyful, creative experience. It can be a calming, healing practice that centers us. Personally I find I have more patience, compassion, and enthusiasm for everything and everyone after a writing session, just as I do after a yoga class, and in that way my writing is also good for my family.

Writing can help us release old stories and write new ones. It can help us get present, pay attention to our lives, appreciate what we have, and stand in awe of the mystery of it all (which is a fantastic antidote to day-to-day worries about things that don't really matter). If we choose to share our words, and they resonate deeply with someone, we strengthen our sense of meaning, belonging, and connection.

But perhaps most important, writing can help us quiet the noise of the modern world, where we are constantly battered by information and other people's opinions, in order to discover what we really think and value. It can help us develop a relationship with ourselves, find our place in the world, and discover what we know deep down to be true, which can have a profound impact on the way we live.

Why does ritual matter?

When we bring ritual into our practice, we can quiet the noise (in our environment, and in our heads) to hear what we really want to say (or more accurately, what wants to be written). We can go beyond scribbling down what we are thinking (when we are aware of what we are doing), into a place where we are fully absorbed in the experience. This is where it gets interesting. It's where we meet the true version of ourselves, which is not necessarily the same version we show to the world. It's where our own inner wisdom is revealed to us, even if we don't know we are carrying that wisdom until we see evidence of it on the page. That might sound a bit "woo," but it's really just the workings of creativity, and ritual can help us get to that place and go deep with our writing.

Tell us a bit about your writing space.

My writing space is my sanctuary. It's a tiny room at the back of the house. We live in a really old cottage that has two staircases, and my room is basically the area under the back stairs but with windows.

My desk is enormous. It takes up nearly half the room. It's a work-bench from an old school science lab. It has a wooden top that's cov-ered in scratches, and on the left, there's a hidden cavity accessible by putting your fingers in a large hole and pulling up a chunk of wood. It's perfect for hiding snacks in. The room has a very old flagstone floor, which is lovely and cool in the summer but in need of a rug in the winter. There's an armchair, and a bookshelf, and not a lot else.

What is on your desk?

My desk is usually clear, but it faces a wall of white shelves where I keep all sorts of bits and pieces that inspire my work. If you visited right now, here are some of the things you would find: an old tea-pot from Kyoto; a bell from the Portland Japanese Garden; a jam jar full of writing prompts; a few favorite mugs holding pens, pencils, paint brushes, scissors, and feathers; a pair of meditation bells joined by a thin strip of leather; a wild gorse candle; a rose and geranium candle; a black pepper candle; some matches; a paper cup covered in scribbles; a tiny vase of flowers; a small globe that spins at an angle; a couple of books of poetry with covers in a calm color; and a chunk of clay one of my daughters fashioned into a heart shape. I can count twenty-three crystals, seventeen notebooks, a diary, and an *omamori,* which is a charm for protection that I got from Meiji Shrine in Tokyo a couple of decades ago. There is a framed picture, some hand cream, an aromatizer and a bunch of essential oils, and a wooden sign that says *What are you waiting for?* There's also an In-stax Polaroid camera, a chipped mug full of receipts, far too much washi tape, and some affirmation cards. It sounds like a lot, but it really isn't. These are all things that I use one way or another in my writing—sometimes in a ritual, perhaps as a memory prompt, or just as reminders of what I came to this desk to do: to write, to practice writing. To write as a sacred practice.

What is your favorite stationery?

I'm not much of a "stuff" person, but I believe that money spent on travel, books, and stationery is never wasted. I have all sorts of stationery, but am most loyal to a few things, including Uniball Eye and Pilot V-Ball black pens, my Hobonichi diary, and notebooks from MD Paper, Leuchtturm1917, and Katie Leamon.

Can you share a peek into your notebooks?

I often change the way I work with notebooks depending on the season or what I'm working on. Sometimes I have a few on the go—one for book ideas, one for business ideas, and so on. Within those notebooks, sometimes my writing is really messy, sometimes it's really neat. Some pages have mind maps. Some pages are long lists of random thoughts or interesting word combinations, tiny sketches or writing exercises that I've done. There are lists of things I want to read or follow up on. Some pages have oracle cards taped in. One page here has forty-six ideas for growing my business, sandwiched in between notes for my next book. And there's a timeline for the lifespans of characters in a secret novel that I haven't written yet.

Some of my notebooks are very neat, but most of them are messy. As I go about my daily life, part of my practice is to pay attention to what interests me and put it all in there. I collect delicious words, write what I notice, keep postcards, scribble maps, make notes of snippets of a conversation, write out my favorite poems. It's fun to do, and later all it takes is a quick flick back through those pages to get a shot of inspiration. If you're a highly visual person, this can make a huge difference in how easily you open your heart and let the words flow.

About the Author

BETH KEMPTON is a Japanologist, self-help author, and writer mentor, whose books have been translated into more than twenty-five languages. Beth has been a student of Japanese life for a quarter of a century, and has two degrees in Japanese. She is also a qualified yoga teacher and a *Reiki* master, trained in the Japanese tradition in Tōkyō.

She has long been a seeker of beauty, and as a writer she uses words to wrangle big questions about how to live well. As a mentor, Beth offers support and inspiration to writers and dreamers, teaching how words and ideas can heal, inspire, uplift, connect, and help us make the most of our time in this beautiful world. Her company, Do What You Love, has delivered original online courses to more than a hundred thousand people, helping them to navigate life, live creatively, and do what they love.

She lives a slow-ish life by the sea in rural Devon, England, with her husband, Mr. K, and their two young girls.

dowhatyouloveforlife.com / bethkempton.com
Instagram @bethkempton
Facebook/Twitter @DoWhatYouLoveXx